Climate Change

Grades 5-8

Written by Darcy J. Gentleman
Illustrated by S&S Learning Materials

About the author:
Darcy J. Gentleman has a Ph.D. in analytical chemistry from Arizona State University. His research focused on developing a fiber optic sensor to monitor the ocean's salt content. Darcy has taught chemistry and writes about the environment and nanotechnology. In August 2008, he became the Managing Editor of the scientific journal *Environmental Science & Technology*.

ISBN 978-1-55495-019-5

Published in the U.S.A by:
On The Mark Press
3909 Witmer Road PMB 175
Niagara Falls, New York
14305
www.onthemarkpress.com

Published in Canada by:
S&S Learning Materials
15 Dairy Avenue
Napanee, Ontario
K7R 1M4
www.sslearning.com

At A Glance

Learning Expectations	Weather and Climate	Measuring Change	The Greenhouse Effect	Heating and Cooling the Earth	The Push and Pull of Climate Change
Understanding concepts					
Understand that weather is day-to-day	•	•		•	•
Understand that climate is the long term average of weather	•	•		•	•
Learn how to detect and measure change	•	•	•	•	•
Recognize patterns and trends in order to predict	•	•	•	•	•
Explain how trapped air heats up upon exposure to light (the greenhouse effect)			•	•	•
Understand and explain how climate change can cause both heating and cooling				•	•
Understand how climate change can alter weather patterns including precipitation	•	•		•	•
Suggest various methods of preparing for and/or minimizing the effects of climate change	•		•	•	•
Skills of inquiry, design, and communication					
Demonstrate an awareness of the scientific method		•	•	•	•
Classify and sort concepts	•	•	•	•	•
Observe with the senses and instruments	•	•	•	•	
Work with others	•	•	•	•	•
Listen, record, and compare others' observations	•	•	•	•	•
Make predictions	•	•	•	•	•
Record observations, findings, and measurements using drawing, tables, and written descriptions	•	•	•	•	•
Communicate the procedure and results of investigations using drawing and written descriptions	•	•	•	•	•
Connect various ideas from observations and previous knowledge to understand new concepts	•	•	•	•	•
Relating science and technology to the outside world					
Relate scientific concepts to objects in their environment	•	•	•	•	•

Table of Contents

Table of Contents

Teacher Assessment Rubric

Student's Name: ______________________________

Criteria	Level 1	Level 2	Level 3	Level 4
Understanding Concepts				
Demonstrated understanding of the basic concepts of climate change	Limited understanding	Some understanding	General understanding	Thorough understanding
Demonstrated misconceptions	Significant misconceptions	Minor misconceptions	No significant misconceptions	No misconceptions
Quality of explanations that were given	Shows limited understanding of concepts	Gives only partial explanations	Usually gives complete or almost complete explanations	Always gives complete and accurate explanations
Inquiry, design and communication skills				
Ability to question, predict, carry out a procedure, observe, and conclude as they relate to the scientific method	Limited ability	Some ability	Good ability	Consistent ability
Use of the correct vocabulary relating to climate change, and precision of communication	Limited communication	Some communication	Good communication	Consistent, effective communication
Awareness and use of safety procedures in the classroom	Limited awareness	Some awareness	Good awareness	Consistent awareness
Relating science and technology to each other and the world outside of school				
Demonstrated understanding of the connection between science and technology of climate change in familiar contexts	Limited understanding	Some understanding	Good understanding	Understanding of connections in familiar and unfamiliar contexts
Demonstrated understanding of the connections between science and technology of climate change and the world	Limited understanding	Some understanding	Good understanding	Understanding of connections and their implications

Student Achievement Rubric

Name: ___________________________________

Individual Work:

4 - I exceeded the objectives of the activity or investigation
3 - I met all of the objectives of the activity or investigation
2 - I met some of the objectives of the activity or investigation but did not meet others
1 - I did not meet the objectives of the activity or investigation
0 - I did not complete the activity or investigation

Activity										
Score										

Group Work:

4 - I helped my group exceed the objectives of the activity or investigation
3 - I helped my group meet the objectives of the activity or investigation
2 - I helped my group a little bit to meet the objectives of the activity or investigation
1 - I barely helped my group at all to meet the objectives of the activity or investigation
0 - I did not help my group in any way

Activity										
Score										
Number of Group Members										
% of work I did										

Student Effort:

4 - I worked on the task to maximum effort
3 - I worked on the task but stopped early
2 - I worked on the task but put very little work into it
1 - I read the task but did not put any work into it
0 - I did not do the task

Activity										
Score										

Introduction

The intent of this workbook is to present students with activities that structure their conceptual understanding of climate change. This is accomplished through a series of hands-on and thought experiments followed by questions to build students' analytical thinking skills. Therefore, whether or not they further pursue science, students – later citizens – will be able to reason through the factors that affect issues of central concern to society, including climate change.

The book is divided into five parts:

Weather and Climate (pages 14 – 22) gets students thinking about the temporal and spatial scale of climates in order to confront the concept of global changes.

Measuring Change (pages 23 – 35) builds students' observational and data analysis skills that will aid in their extracting meaning from the subsequent experiments and concept-teaching questions. This section will be of use to any curricular content for which tracking change is necessary.

The Greenhouse Effect (pages 36 – 54) focuses on the dominant issue of present concern for climate change. While certainly not the only issue, the groundswell of attention garnered by global warming means that a generation of students will need to understand this concept that is already driving social change. Every effort was made to present the effect accurately without complicating its explanation. The intent is for students to "discover" the greenhouse effect as opposed to blindly applying dogmatic knowledge in token demonstrations. Myriad studies in science education have shown that an inquiry/discovery approach allows students to take ownership of their learned knowledge while building scientific skills. Once they have developed their own comprehension of how greenhouses work, the conceptualization of infrared radiation interacting with atmospheric molecules will be better retained. Note that a detailed explanation is beyond the scope of this book.

Heating and Cooling the Earth (pages 55 – 73) combines the first three parts and has students begin to apply their accrued knowledge. Much of these activities and thought experiments concern water and ice, as that is where the lion's share of evidence for present climate change exists. Class discussions upon completing the activities can therefore be well augmented by current affairs.

The Push and Pull of Climate Change (pages 74 – 86) collates students' abstract thinking skills to synthesize their fundamental understanding of climate change. The activities encourage debate and prediction within the context of global warming. Students will therefore be better able to weigh risks and propose solutions to myriad problems, both generally and specifically to climate change.

It is hoped that in using this resource to augment your lessons, students will come away with the ability to problem solve and think critically rather than regurgitate countless facts. Climate change has occurred and continues to take place; today's students need to be prepared to make the most of our future.

Teacher Notes

Within the text, the phrase "classroom resources" refers to books, media, and Internet resources. Some of the activities refer to diagrams found on the World Wide Web that accurately show the present and predicted conditions of Earth's climate(s). An effort was made to use authoritative sources such as NASA and NOAA. In directing students to web-based sources, it is vital that their informational literacy is developed and they understand the need to check multiple sources.

The following annotations are to aid your delivery of the activities, and should be considered in concert with the detailed answers given in the Answer Key.

Climates of the World (page 16): Give students the weather of their destination city for the same week the prior year. At least one group should have an unexpected result, such as a resort that had a major storm the prior year.

Weather Patterns Make Climates (page 19): Permanent marker washes off glass with acetone (nail polish remover).

Any time "plants" are mentioned, geraniums are an excellent choice – they are inexpensive and hardy.

Measuring Change (page 23): Class discussion on "opinion" versus "observation" of change. If fire regulations forbid open flames, omit the candle experiment.

Short Term and Long Term Change (page 27): Groups should be assigned different classrooms. Tell students to be truthful with subjects if asked; students then comment on how the response changed once the information was public. In class discussions, introduce the concept of long term showing the "big picture".

Temperature Trends (page 29): Question 6 concerning "centuries of data" confronts the nuance of a "changing average". This would make for a good discussion with advanced students.

Watering Changes (page 33): To determine volume of water, again, geraniums are the best choice.

1. Pour measured volume of water into the potted plant's saucer.
2. Let sit until the **top** of the soil is moist to the touch.
3. Measure the amount left in the saucer (add more water until some remains).
4. Difference in amount remaining from amount added is volume to use for "normal".

Can We Control Climate? (page 37): Refrigerator removes hot air – **it does not "add" cold air**. Class discussion that **heat moves**. **The absence of heat is "cold".**

Greenhouse Experiments (pages 39 – 54): In general, see the reference in the bibliography by S.B. Lueddecke, *et al*. There are myriad greenhouse experiments/demonstrations available on the web and in various books. It is best to experiment with the set up prior to using them, as times and type of lighting may affect results. There is some debate as to whether glass or plastic tops are best, this will always depend on the materials. Thick construction plastic will work well, especially given its translucency. If you are so inclined, a box constructed of wood could be used as well, but cardboard is sufficient and permits the students to gain the satisfaction of constructing the models themselves. Using the window to insert the thermometer/hygrometer will disturb the air and may permit humidity or carbon dioxide (CO_2) to escape – using digital readers with remote probes could alleviate this issue. Multiple greenhouses can be constructed for any experiment to save class time.

Teacher Notes

Clouds Over the Greenhouse (page 41): Try to use plastics that have similar textures, otherwise their composition will affect the results in addition to their color. If this is unavoidable, point out this fact to the students and use it to lead a class discussion on experimental variables.

Greenhouses are Traps (page 43): An alternative could be to tape cardboard on the sides of a terrarium.

Humidity (pages 45 – 48): This experiment ties in well with curricular states of matter/phase changes. Note that hurricane winds are revved up by the heat that is given off by water vapor condensing into clouds. Global warming literally fuels such storms.

A digital hygrometer is easier to use than this wet bulb hygrometer (also called a *psychrometer*), and will display relative humidity (RH).

RH = amount of water vapor in air/amount of water vapor air can hold

RH is usually reported as a percentage, which is calculated simply by multiplying the above ratio by 100%. RH is dependent on temperature – warm air holds more water vapor. The corollary is that the cooling sensation on skin upon emerging from a pool is more dramatic when the air is warm. The general lack of people swimming in the winter means most do not experience the lesser effect. However, speaking to this can flare out the discussion with the students.

Kitty litter is a reasonable wick for air moisture (a *desiccant*) but hardly the best. Silica gel (bagged beads packed with electronics and other consumer products) is better, as is Drierite (calcium sulfate). Plaster of Paris is dehydrated gypsum, which could also work. However as these are "chemicals" they may introduce safety issues that you do not wish to confront, in addition to their cost.

Carbon Dioxide and Greenhouses (page 51): **Experiment with this set up prior to use. Read Lueddecke *et al.*, especially notes on "Results, Warnings, and Variations."** It is crucial that the glasses chosen are tall enough to contain the foam produced by the baking soda. The amount used here is excessive in order to produce a significant amount of CO_2, but feel free to modify the recipe.

Take special note of Lueddecke *et al.*'s remark that adding new baking soda will cause *cooling* due to the chemical reaction's energetics. Repeated tests of the version here did find cooling with time, but in the first 10 minutes there was at least 1.5 °C of warming. As noted in Lueddecke *et al*, use of a glass top, or none at all given that CO_2 is heavier than air, may increase the differential.

It is not recommended to use dry ice unless you can rig a way of pumping its off-gassing into the chamber. Dry ice in the greenhouse model will surely cool it so as to not see the effect. Further, the "smoke" which is actually water vapor flash freezing will reflect light and cause further cooling.

The Color of Earth/Will The Earth Heat Evenly? (pages 55 and 56): The monochromatic printing of this workbook limits these maps' legibility. Paper-based photographs in books may also work. If links listed herein cease to work, both NASA and NOAA continually update such information. You may need to lead a class discussion of using color to convey information on a map.

Teacher Notes

Water and Ice and Heat (page 58): *An Inconvenient Truth* has an excellent illustration of this phenomenon starting at time index 41:50.

Feedback (page 60): Without going into mathematical rigor, the reason the curve shows more dramatic change than a straight line should be addressed in class discussion. Also, a discussion on the nature of permafrost can emerge from this activity.

Moving Water in the Oceans (page 64): Dyes in a fish tank also show convection currents, but will dissipate quickly. The listed web sites range in difficulty; feel free to add others you encounter in finalizing your lesson plan that best speak to your particular students.

Changing the Current (page 66): Depending on the size of the carpet swatch and the patience of your students, you may need to adjust the timings/method. The carpet is meant to control the marbles' movement (use twill, not shag!) but a hard surface would work for a quick demonstration. *An Inconvenient Truth* speaks to the Gulf Stream starting around time index 41:50.

Rising Seas and Shores (page 68): *An Inconvenient Truth* shows this predicted effect from time index 57:30 – 1:01:10. A possible class discussion topic is a debate of what to do in the face of *modeled* predictions.

Glaciers and Sea Level (page 71): As noted, *An Inconvenient Truth* illustrates this well.

Relative Impact (page 74): Tie in with states of matter/phase changes. Could note that a small cup of hot water has a higher temperature than a bucket of warm water, but the latter has more **heat**. Therefore the bucket gives up less heat when melting the ice and sees a smaller temperature change. This is also a tie in for "lake effect snow" in regions where this topic is included in the curriculum.

Local Affects Global (page 76): After completing the activity as written, students can modify the station tasks as an exercise in experimental design. Also, students good with computers could be tasked with creating an electronic version. If so, ensure they are attuned to resources on climate modeling.

The Push and Pull of Climate Change (pages 74-85): This entire section contains questions that are highly conducive to group and/or class discussions. In particular:

- Natural and Artificial (page 78) question 4
- Sources and Sinks (page 79) question 6
- Debating Pollution (page 81) question 4
- *An Inconvenient Truth* (page 83) Graphing question 5
- Are Clouds Good or Bad? (page 84) question 5
- Cities and Climate (page 85) question 10

References

This page provides bibliographic references. The present attention paid to climate change in the popular and technical media means that this is far from a complete list. The four sources listed below are particularly useful for directing you to more content that could be adapted within the more conceptual activities of this workbook:

- *The Rough Guide to Climate Change* – The first edition of this book was shortlisted by Britain's Royal Society for its Science Books award.
- *The Cartoon Guide to the Environment* – Gonick is a first-rate nonfiction cartoonist.
- *We Are the Weather Makers* – Tim Flannery's own revision of his critically acclaimed *The Weather Makers*, intended "for readers age twelve and up."
- *An Inconvenient Truth* – Time indices listed in the activities focus on the science content. This film is an excellent introduction to climate change and accessible to all.

Bibliography

Flannery, T. (2005). *The Weather Makers*. Toronto: HarperCollins.

Flannery, T. (2006). *We Are the Weather Makers*. Toronto: HarperCollins.

Gonick, L. & Outwater, A. (1996). *The Cartoon Guide to the Environment*. New York: HarperCollins.

Guggenheim, D., Director. (2006). *An Inconvenient Truth*. Hollywood: Paramount Pictures.

Harris, D.C. (2003). *Quantitative Chemical Analysis*. New York: W.H. Freeman and Company.

Henson, R. (2007). *The Rough Guide to Weather, 2e*. New York: Rough Guides Ltd., Penguin Group.

Ince, M. (2007). *The Rough Guide to the Earth*. New York: Rough Guides Ltd., Penguin Group.

Lueddecke, S.B., Pinter, N., & McManus, S.A. (2001). "Greenhouse effect in the classroom: a project – and laboratory – based curriculum." *Journal of Geoscience Education*, **49**(3), 274-279.

Lynch, J. (2002). *The Weather*. Toronto: Firefly Books Ltd.

McKeever, S., ed. (1998). *The DK Science Encyclopedia*. New York: DK Publishing, Inc.

Internet References

www.nasa.gov

www.noaa.gov

http://weathereye.kgan.com/lounge/index.html

http://www.weatherwizkids.com/WxExperiments.htm

http://phet.colorado.edu/simulations/sims.php?sim=The_Greenhouse_Effect

http://www.sciencebuddies.org/science-fair-projects/project_ideas/Weather_p011.shtml

http://www.sciencenews.org/view/feature/id/31477/title/Science_News_for_Kids_Polar_Ice_Feels_the_Heat

http://www.bbc.co.uk/sn/hottopics/climatechange/moreaboutexperiment.shtml

http://nicholasacademy.com/scienceexperiment215meltingicebergs.html

http://www.nagt.org/files/nagt/jge/abstracts/Lueddecke_v49n3p274.pdf

Materials

Consumables

- aluminum foil
- baking soda
- black construction paper
- candle at least 3” (7.5 cm) wide
- candle no more than 1” (2.5 cm) wide
- cardboard boxes at least 12” (30 cm) on each side
- plastic wrap (clear, black, blue, green, red, white, yellow)
- cotton batting (or torn up cotton balls)
- elastic bands
- green plants (e.g., geraniums)
- ice cubes
- kitty litter
- match or a lighter
- nylon socks
- bread
- paper towel or wrapping paper tube
- Plasticine
- salt
- small pasta shells or rice
- vinegar
- water – chilled from refrigerator, lukewarm, hot, boiling

Non-Consumables

- 9” x 13” (23 x 33 cm) baking pan, preferably glass
- air conditioner in window
- air conditioner situated outside (optional)
- alarm clock
- blankets/sheets of white, green, brown,
- dark blue
- bowls
- bucket
- hot plate
- clock with a second hand or a stopwatch
- cutting board
- desk lamp or sunlight
- dry cloth
- flower vase
- funnel with mouth wider than glass
- glass jar with a lid
- glass plate
- heat resistant glass bowl or pot (coffee pot)
- humidifier or steam source
- hygrometer
- kettle
- large plastic garbage bag
- map of school or home
- marker
- measuring cup
- measuring spoon
- paper
- pie plate
- red and blue marbles
- refrigerator
- roll of masking tape
- ruler
- scissors
- sponge
- square of carpet – about 4.5 sq ft (0.5 m^2)
- tall cup or drinking glass
- tape

Vocabulary

As you use this book, you will come across these words. Define them in your own words. Add any others you learned while using this book.

artificial ______________________________

atmosphere ______________________________

carbon dioxide (CO_2) ______________________________

climate ______________________________

climate control ______________________________

climatologist ______________________________

current ______________________________

environment ______________________________

feedback ______________________________

fluid ______________________________

glaciers ______________________________

global warming ______________________________

greenhouse ______________________________

humidity ______________________________

hygrometer ______________________________

ice pack ______________________________

meteorologist ______________________________

natural ______________________________

pollution ______________________________

sea level ______________________________

sink ______________________________

source ______________________________

trend line ______________________________

weather ______________________________

weather conditions ______________________________

____

____

What is Weather?

Weather is what happens in the air, or the atmosphere, day-to-day. Write down what the weather is for a whole week using the words below. If you do not know what the words mean, use classroom resources to help you find out.

rain
snow
freezing rain
sleet
hail
stormy
sunny
cloudy
partly sunny
partly cloudy
dry
windy
hot – give the temperature
cold – give the temperature
humid

Results:

Day 1	Day 2	Day 3	Day 4	Day 5

Questions:

1. Were the words above enough to describe all of the weather? What else did you use?

____

____

2. Compare your results to a newspaper or internet forecast. Did you agree? Why or why not?

____

____

____

Climates of the World

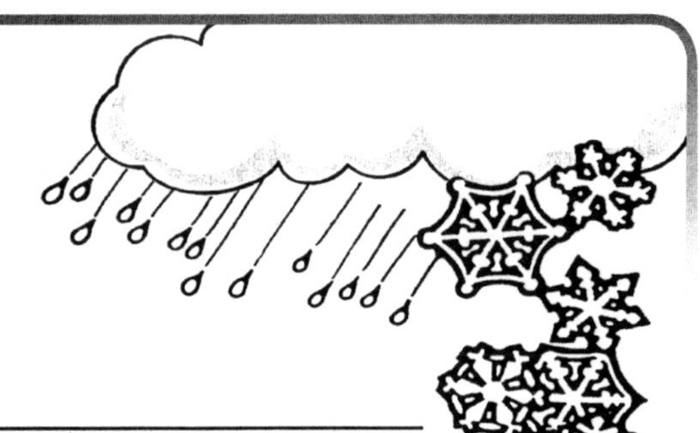

1. a) Pretend it is July 15. Will you need a coat outside? ____________________
   b) Pretend it is January 15. Will you need a coat outside? ____________________
   c) How do you know? ____________________

We know that summer is hot and winter is cold. This is true of our climate. Day-to-day changes in conditions like temperature, precipitation (rain, snow), or wind, are weather. A climate is how the weather averages over many years. Climates can be generally described as hot, cold, wet, or dry. Other conditions like sunny or windy may also describe a climate. Usually a place's climate is a combination: tropical rain forests are hot and wet, mountain tops are often cold and dry.

We have different clothes for different climates to keep comfortable and healthy. You can see this if you look at what people around the world wear. For example, northern fishery workers wear raincoats and warm sweaters. Surfers in California wear shorts and sandals. Desert dwellers wear hats and loose clothing. Make a list of clothing that would be suitable for the climates listed below.

2. a) **Hot** ____________________
   b) **Cold** ____________________
   c) **Wet** ____________________
   d) **Dry** ____________________
   e) **Sunny** ____________________
   f) **Windy** ____________________

Climates of the World

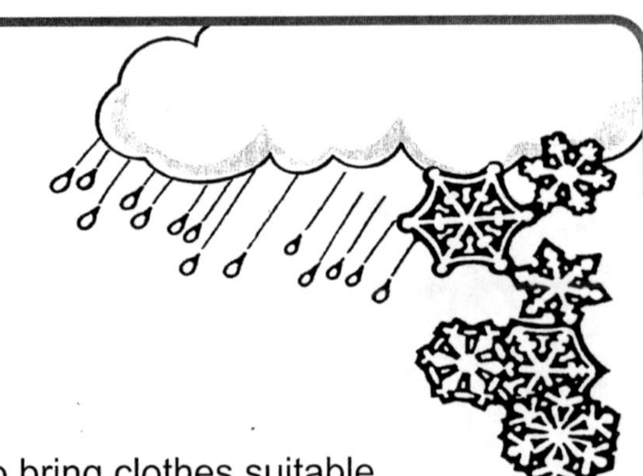

Packing for a Trip:

3. When you are traveling to a different place, you have to bring clothes suitable for its climate. Can you think of ways to figure out a place's climate?

4. In groups or on your own, choose a city or destination from the list provided by your teacher. Imagine that you are going to visit there for all of next week. What clothing should you pack?

Questions:

5. Your teacher will give you some information on your destination. Check your answers. How well prepared for your trip were you? What changes would you make?

6. In the introduction, it was said that you would need a coat in the winter but not the summer. Will this always be true? Explain your answer.

7. What is the best way to plan for a trip? Explain your answer.

Weather or Climate?

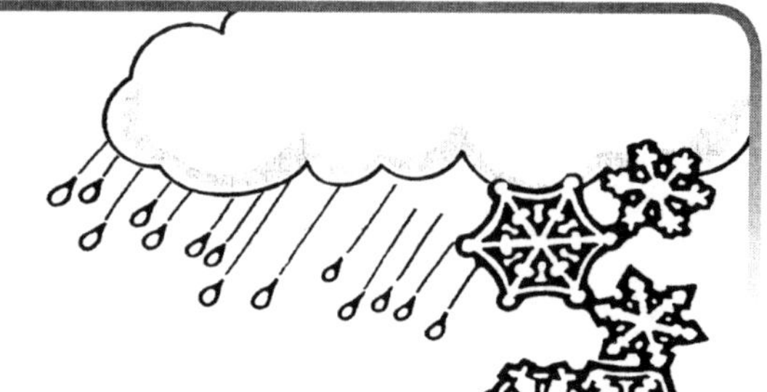

What will it be like outside on a given day? Weather is what happens day-to-day. Climate is the average of weather over long periods of time. Also, the climate of a place will depend on where it is in the world. For example, places near the equator have hot climates, and places near the poles are cold.

Some of the statements below are about weather – put a 'W' in the box next to them. Others are about climate – put a 'C' in the box next to them. Some might be both – write 'WC' next to them.

	The year 1976 was one of the coldest winters on record.
	The year 1992 was one of the coldest summers on record.
	Cities near the ocean tend to be wet.
	Florida is hotter than Alaska.
	It might snow in Florida tomorrow.
	El Niño warms the ocean west of Peru every few years.
	In 1998, two scientists reported that it rains more on weekends on the east coast of the USA.
	It rained on October 10.
	It rains every October.
	It is supposed to be sunny in Phoenix next week.
	It is supposed to rain this weekend.
	The daytime high was 32°F (0°C).
	The normal daytime high is 40°F (5°C).
	Today it was colder than usual.
	Last week was hotter than this week.
	La Niña cools the ocean west of Peru every few years.
	Libya is a hot country.
	Northern Africa is hot.
	November is usually cloudy.
	On July 4, 1956, it rained 1.23" (31.2 mm) in one minute in Unionville, MD.
	Parts of the Atacama Desert in Chile can go several years without rain.
	Phoenix, AZ, can have over 300 days of sun a year.
	Sometimes it snows in late April.
	It is a La Niña year, so I guess it will snow a lot next week.
	Summer is hot.
	The highest recorded temperature of all time was 136°F (58°C), in Libya.
	The lowest recorded temperature for Africa was -11°F (-24°C) in Morocco.
	Winter is cold.
	Yesterday it was cold, so it will probably be cold today.

Weather or Climate?

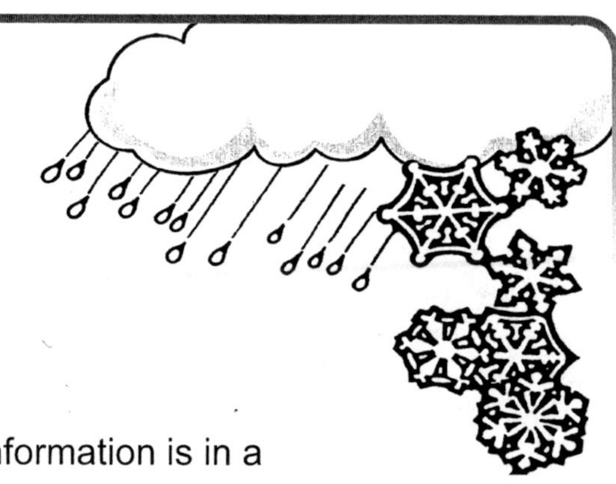

Questions:

1. Compare statements with similar words. What kind of information is in a weather statement? In a climate statement?

____

____

____

2. Draw a picture in the space below that shows the difference between weather and climate.

3. Libya and Morocco are both in northern Africa. Look at the statements about these countries and northern Africa. Explain how all the statements can be true. Use classroom resources including a map to help you answer the question.

____

____

____

____

4. Which would be more surprising: a sudden change in the weather, or a sudden change in the climate? Explain.

____

____

____

____

Weather Patterns Make Climates

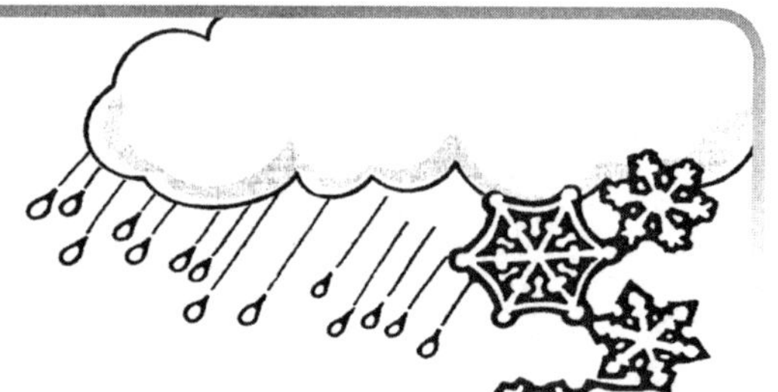

Weather is day-to-day changes. Climate is the average of these changes over a long time. This means lots of days of weather have to be measured to figure out climate. Sometimes early patterns will look nothing like the long term patterns. For example, if you measure the temperature only in the winter, you may think that the climate is very cold. If you measure rainfall during a storm, you may think that the climate is very wet.

Before further exploring climate, measure some weather to see what patterns exist.

Equipment:

- two tall glasses with straight sides
- funnel with mouth wider than glass
- permanent marker
- ruler
- Plasticine

Procedure:

funnel →
Plasticine →
glass →

Make a Rain/Snow Gauge

1. Using the ruler, mark off each 1/8" (2 mm) going up the glass at least 6" (15 cm).
2. Put the funnel over the top of the glass. Secure it with the Plasticine.
3. Place the rain gauge outside.
4. For one week, measure the height of water in the gauge **at the same time every day**. Empty the glass after measuring.

For Snow:

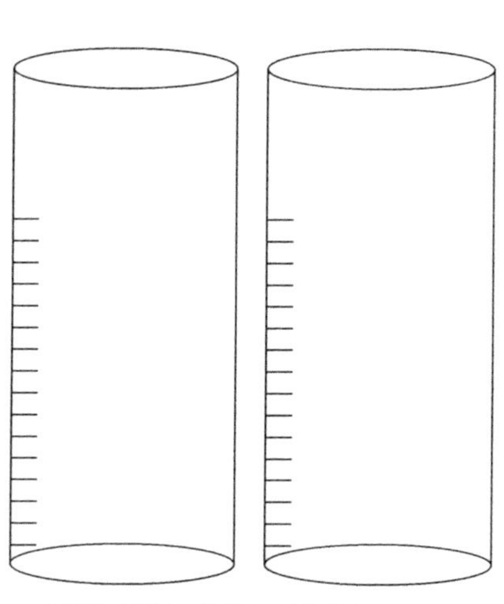

1. Using the ruler, mark off each 1/8" (2 mm) going up the glass at least 6" (15 cm). Do this with **two glasses**.
2. Place the snow gauge outside (no funnel).
3. For one week, measure the height of snow in the gauge **at the same time every day**. Replace the measured glass with the other empty one.
4. Melt the snow completely to water then measure the height of the water.

Use the next page to collect and graph your data.

Weather Patterns Make Climates

	Day 1	Day 2	Day 3	Day 4	Day 5
Rainwater (in/mm)					
Snow (in/mm)					
Melted Snow (in/mm)					

Plot your results using a **bar graph**. Remember to label your graph!

Questions:

1. Looking at your graph, do you live in a wet or dry climate? Explain.

____

____

2. Is the above question fair? Explain.

____

____

Weather Patterns Make Climates

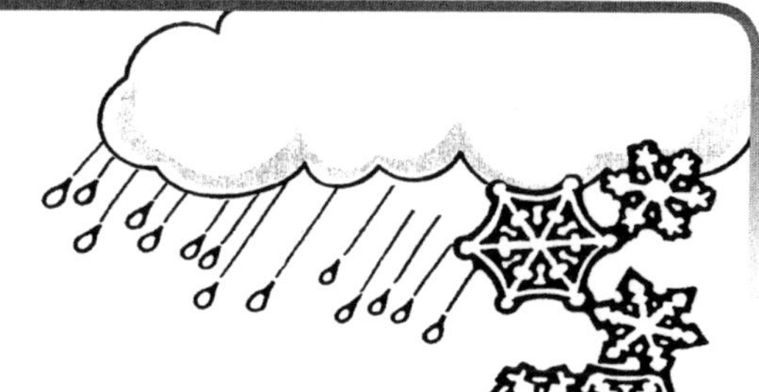

Find precipitation values in your area for all 21 days before you started measuring. Make a new graph including the previous measurements with your results (26 days total).

3. Looking at the graph above, do you live in a wet or dry climate? Explain. ____________________

4. Is the above question fair? Explain. ____________________

5. Using classroom resources, find out the average precipitation for the month that most overlaps with your results: ____________________

6. Compare this average to the results for that month for the previous 30 years. Based on this information, do you live in a wet or dry climate? Explain. ____________________

7. Is the above question fair to decide what climate you live in? Explain. ____________________

Ask an Expert

As a class, meet with a local weather expert. They may be a meteorologist with a local news organization, government center, airport, or university. These experts use measurements to predict the weather day to day. Another kind of expert is a climatologist. These experts study what climates have done over history and predict how they may change. Ask the expert the following questions:

How does the expert measure the weather to decide what climate you live in?

____

____

Is there anything weird about the local weather or climate?

____

____

What training did the expert need to become a meteorologist or climatologist?

____

____

What technology helps with weather forecasting or climate modeling?

____

____

Write down some of your own questions for the expert and include the answers given.

____

____

____

____

____

____

____

____

____

____

Draft a thank you letter to the expert. After your teacher checks it, mail your letter with your classmates' to the expert.

Measuring Change

Change is the process of becoming different. You can measure change by observing objects or systems that become different over time. You can then compare how long each takes to become different. In this experiment, you will measure change over time. This will give you a better idea of what change is and how to measure it.

Materials:

- kettle and water or hot water from a tap
- cup
- thermometer
- dry cloth
- green plant with lots of leaves (e.g., geranium)
- one piece of bread
- glass jar with a lid
- glass plate
- candle at least 3" (7.5 cm) wide
- candle no more than 1" (2.5 cm) wide
- match or a lighter
- clock with a second hand or a stopwatch

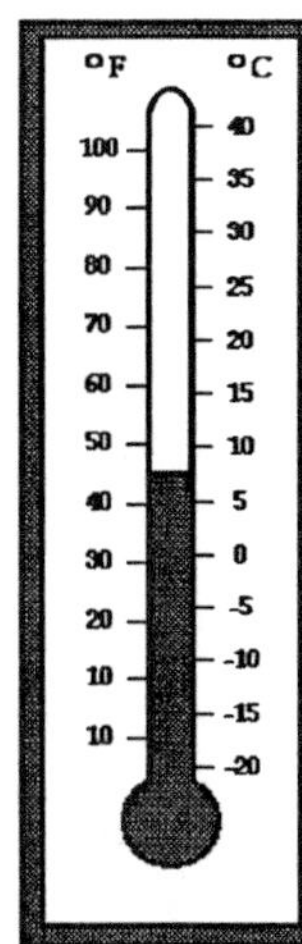

Method:

Match the amount of time with its description word:

FAST •	• hours
MEDIUM •	• minutes or less
SLOW •	• days or more

In groups, make up a method to measure how long these processes take:

1. hot water cooling to room temperature
2. leaves of a plant turning towards sunlight
3. dust collecting on the surface of a glass plate
4. bread in a jar growing mold
5. wet cloth drying
6. pavement warming in the sun (or cooling in the shade)

Have your teacher approve the method before starting the experiments. Measure how long the change takes for each of the six processes. Write the name of each process in the table on the next page based on how long they take to change.

Measuring Change

Measure the starting height of both candles. Have your teacher light the candles and let them burn for one hour. **Be very careful around the flame.** Measure the new height of the candles.

Results:

FAST	MEDIUM	SLOW

Starting height of wide candle ________ Starting height of narrow candle________

Final height of wide candle __________ Final height of narrow candle _________

Questions:

1. How did you determine when the experiment was done? Did any of the experiments keep going? ____

____

2. Is it possible to tell the difference between really slow change and no change? Explain.

____

____

3. Look at the results for the candles. Did they change the same amount? Which changed more? ____

4. Both candles burned for one hour and both are made of the same wax. What measurement could you make that would show they changed the same amount?

____

____

5. Two people can look at the same thing and see different amounts of change. How is this possible? ____

Ideas of Change

Do different people measure time differently? One way is to find out how much they think things change. In this survey, you will ask people of different ages how much they think "times have changed". Then you can report if someone's age affects how they measure time.

Method:

Ask one person in each of three age groups all eight questions. Write the answers in the spaces.

"Since you were nine years old, how much has changed in any of the following?

your neighborhood
fashion
price of candy
your friends

music
traffic
price of a movie
the climate

Answers:

Person 10 – 21 years old

____
____
____
____
____
____
____

Person 22 – 50 years old

____
____
____
____
____
____
____

Ideas of Change

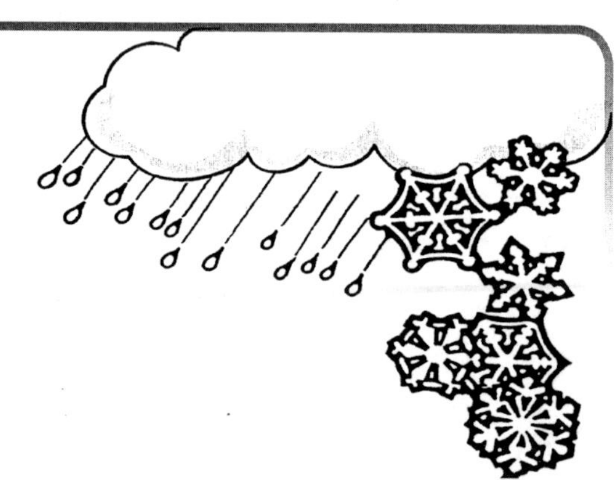

Person over 50 years old

Questions (for you):

Compare your results with the rest of your class.

1. Which age group noticed the least amount of change? Which group noticed the most? Explain why you think this is.

2. Which age group had the most different answers from person to person? Why do you think this is?

3. Combine the answers from your class for the climate question. Which age group has seen more change? Do any age groups think nothing has changed?

4. If you were measuring climate change over a period of ten years, which age group would be the best to use? Explain your answer.

Short Term Change and Long Term Change

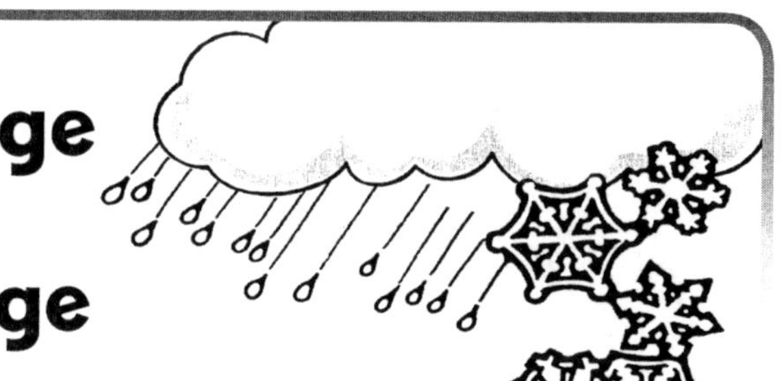

The change over a short amount of time can be very different to the change over a long amount of time. Sometimes the change can even reverse direction. For example, it can get cold over a week in January but then be much warmer in July. In this experiment, you are going to observe change in people's eating habits and compare the short and long term changes.

Method:

Your teacher will assign you a group of people to observe. Every day for one week, go to that group at their lunch time. Count the number of apples the group has to eat on that day. Record your data in the chart below.

Results:

Day	Number of Apples
1.	
2.	
3.	
4.	
5.	

Using the axes below, draw a point for each day. Remember to label your graph!

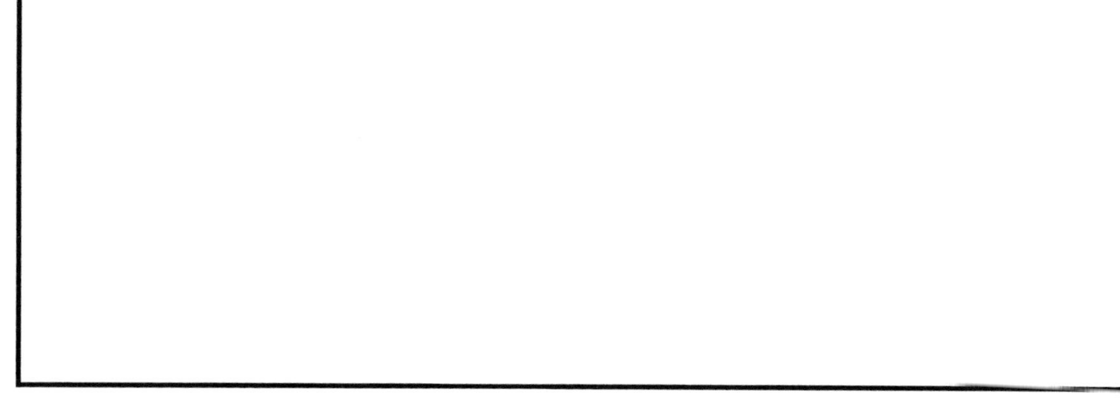

Seeing Change

Draw straight connecting lines from point to point. Then, using a ruler, draw **one** straight line that gets as close to every point as possible. This a **trend line**. Look at the examples for help:

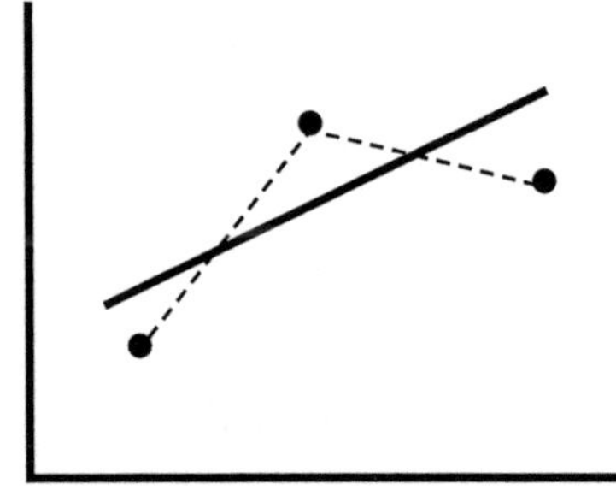

CORRECT

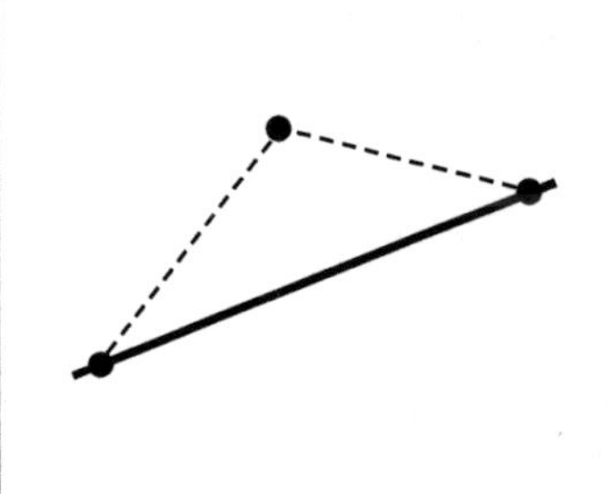

INCORRECT

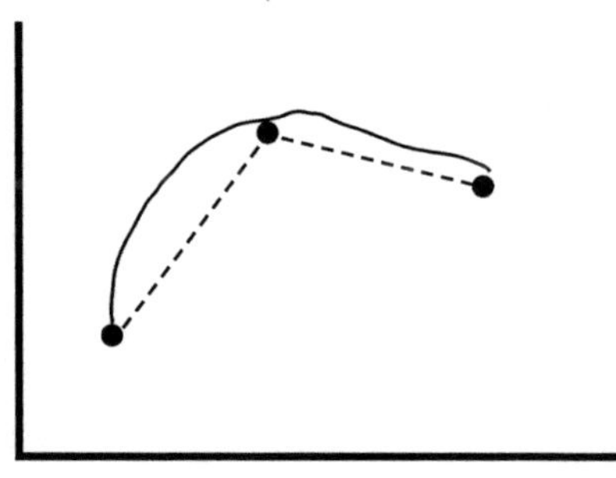

INCORRECT

Questions:

1. What day-to-day change was the smallest? What was the overall change? Are they the same? Explain.

____

____

____

2. We call the day-to-day change "short term" change, and the overall change "long term" change. Using your observations, explain why these are good descriptors.

____

____

3. Trend lines help us to see "real" change. Explain why, using the example shown below.

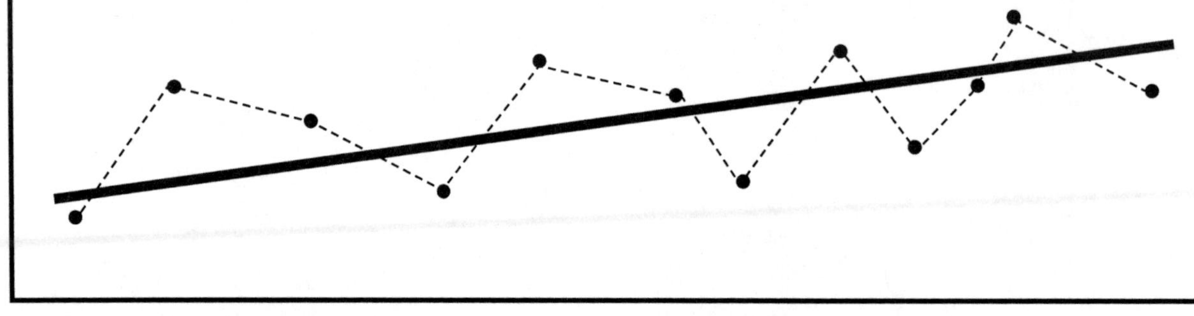

____

____

Temperature Trends

Does temperature change over time? It is usually cooler in the morning and warms up over the day. It is hotter in the summer and colder in the winter. But is the temperature changing from year to year? Using your own measurements and information from a weather service, you can see if this is true.

Materials: ✪ thermometer ✪ alarm clock

Method:

Set the alarm clock to go off at the same time every day for five days. At this time, measure the outside temperature. **The thermometer should be 5 ft (1.5 m) above the ground, in the shade, in the same place every day**. Put the results in the table below.

Results:

Day	Time	Temperature (°F or °C)
1		
2		
3		
4		
5		

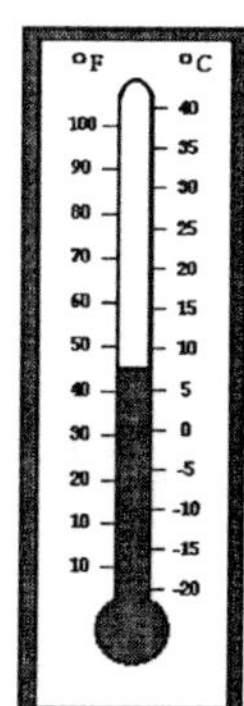

Plot the temperature for the week using the axes below. Remember to label and title your graph! Draw a trend line.

Historical Temperatures

Using your local weather service, plot out the temperature in your area for the same set of days one year ago, five years ago, 10 years ago, and 20 years ago. Draw a trend line for each.

Average Change

Add together the temperatures for each of the five days:

temp 1 __________ + temp 2 _________+ temp 3 _________ + temp 4 ________ + temp 5 _________ = temp total ______. Divide this answer by 5: temp total ÷ 5 = ______ **This is the average temperature for the week.**

Using information from the weather service, calculate the week's average every year for the last 20 years. Plot these averages on the axes below. Draw a trend line. Then answer the questions.

average temperature (°F or °C)

Year

Questions:

1. What would the trend line look like if nothing changes? If the change is big? If it were getting warmer? If it were getting cooler?____

____

____

2. a) Define weather: ____

____

b) Define climate: ____

____

3. Do the trend lines on the week long graphs show weather or climate? What about on the graph of averages? Explain.____

____

____

Average Change

4. Look only at the week long graphs. Can you tell from the trend lines if the climate is changing? Explain.

5. Look only at the graph of averages. Can you tell from the trend line if the climate is changing? Explain.

6. Scientists use hundreds of years (centuries) of temperature information (data) to figure out if climate is changing. Explain why.

7. Look at the graph below:

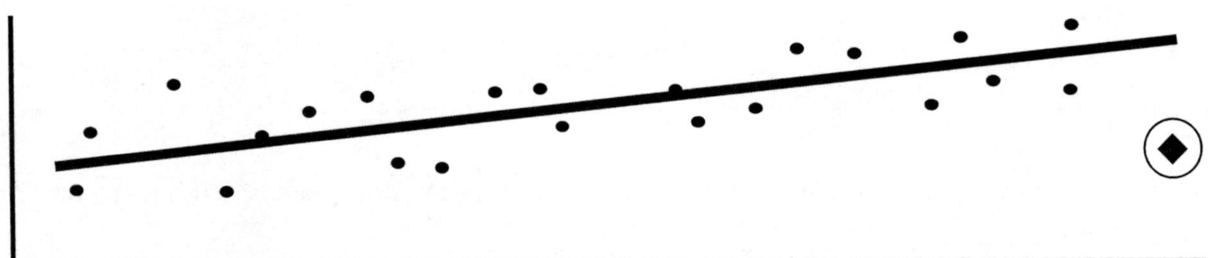

a) Look at the diamond in the circle. What does the graph say about that year's weather?

b) Does the graph show climate change? Explain.

c) Draw a new trend line to include the circled point. Does the graph show climate change?

Watering Changes

One effect of climate change is that regions may experience different precipitation conditions. A "normal" climate could become very wet or very dry. Also, the speed of change could be slow or fast. What effect do you think this will have on plants? In this experiment, you will find out.

Materials:

- nine potted plants (geraniums are good)
- water
- measuring cup
- ruler
- string

Method:

This experiment has two phases. Phase 1 sets up the watering conditions and Phase 2 changes them.

Your teacher will tell you how much water is "normal" based on the plants you are using. To determine if a plant is healthy, measure its height every week and the distance around its leaves using the string. Some plants may have color changes as well. Put all of this data in the table.

After reading **ALL** the directions, predict which plants will be the healthiest and which will be the unhealthiest. Be sure to **label** the plants!

Phase 1	For **three straight weeks:**
Plant A	Gets the normal volume of water **once per week.**
Plant B	Gets **no water**.
Plant C	Gets the normal volume of water **three times per week.**
Plant D	Gets **no water**.
Plant E	Gets the normal volume of water **three times per week**.
Plant F	Gets **no water**.
Plant G	Gets the normal volume of water **three times per week**.
Plant H	Gets the normal volume of water **once per week**.
Plant I	Gets the normal volume of water **once per week**.

Phase 2	For **three straight weeks:** (bringing the experiment to six weeks long):
Plant A	Gets the normal volume of water **once per week**.
Plant B	Gets **no water**.
Plant C	Gets the normal volume of water **three times per week**.
Plant D	Gets the normal volume of water **once per week**.
Plant E	Gets the normal volume of water **once per week**.
Plant F	Gets the normal volume of water **three times per week**.
Plant G	Gets **no water**.
Plant H	Gets **no water**.
Plant I	Gets the normal volume of water **three times per week**.

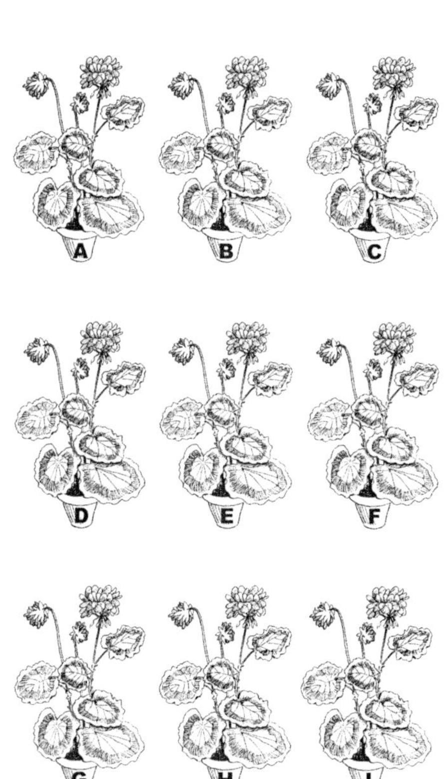

Watering Changes

Prediction for healthiest plant: ______________________________

Prediction for unhealthiest plant: ______________________________

Results:

Plant	Observations	Start	Week 1	Week 2	Week 3	Week 4	Week 5	Week 6
A	height (in/cm)							
	circumference (in/cm)							
	appearance							
B	height (in/cm)							
	circumference (in/cm)							
	appearance							
C	height (in/cm)							
	circumference (in/cm)							
	appearance							
D	height (in/cm)							
	circumference (in/cm)							
	appearance							
E	height (in/cm)							
	circumference (in/cm)							
	appearance							
F	height (in/cm)							
	circumference (in/cm)							
	appearance							
G	height (in/cm)							
	circumference (in/cm)							
	appearance							
H	height (in/cm)							
	circumference (in/cm)							
	appearance							
I	height (in/cm)							
	circumference (in/cm)							
	appearance							

Watering Changes

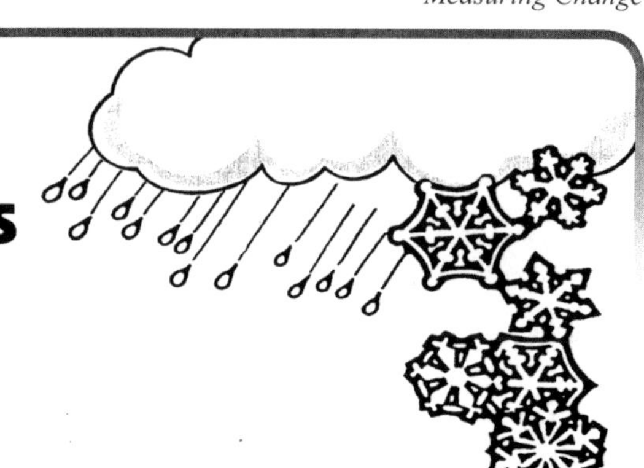

Questions:

1. Which plants survived? Which are the healthiest? Which are the unhealthiest? Did any die? How do the results compare to your predictions?

____

____

2. Which plants had the greatest change over the six weeks? Which had the least change over the six weeks?

____

____

3. Based on your results, what are the best watering instructions for these plants? What are the worst instructions?

____

____

4. Which has more change between increasing and decreasing watering? Do these results make sense to you? Explain.

____

____

5. If all plants are like the ones you used, which is more harmful: sudden change or slow change? Use your results to explain your answer.

____

____

____

6. If climate change causes different rain cycles, what should we do to figure out how to save plants? ____

____

____

____

Air Inventory

Buildings keep constant temperature and humidity by using "climate control". Heaters, air conditioners, windows, and insulation move and trap air to keep the indoors comfortable. In this activity, you will take an inventory of the air in your school and/or home.

Materials:
- thermometer
- map of school or home

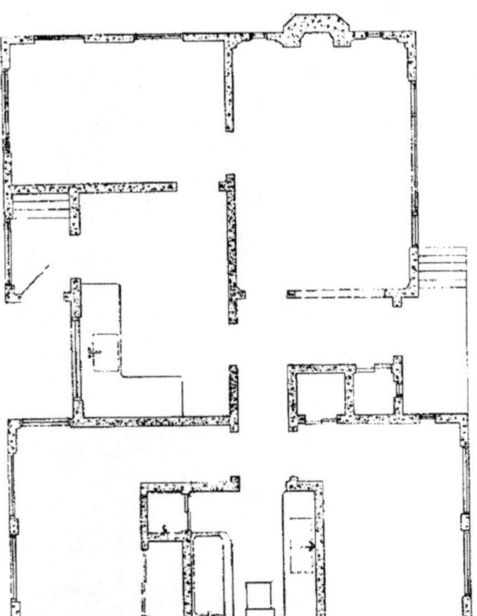

Method:

1. Measure the temperature in the middle of every room. If there is a vent, a window, or a door, take the temperature next to it as well.

2. Measure the temperatures outside at each corner of the building. If there are any vents, air conditioners, or areas of windows and doors, take measurements there, too.

3. Write all of your measurements on your map.

4. Wait for a day when the outside temperature is very different from the day you first measured. Repeat steps 1-3. Write the results in a different color or circle them on your map.

Questions:

1. When the temperature changes a lot outside, how do the temperatures inside change? Do all rooms and positions change equally? Do any stay the same? Explain your answers.

____

____

____

2. How did the temperature near a vent change when the outside temperature was different? What reasons may explain your observations? ______________________________

____

3. If climate change causes the outside temperature to change a lot, will the inside be changed? Explain why. ______________________________________

____

Can We Control Climate?

Climate outside occurs naturally. Indoors, we use machines to keep constant temperature and call it "climate control." Air conditioners make places cooler when it is hot outside. But do air conditioners really make everything cooler? This activity will help you figure that out.

Materials:

- thermometer
- refrigerator
- window with no air conditioner
- window with air conditioner
- outside air conditioner unit

Method:

On a day that it is hotter outside than inside:

1. Go to a window that has no air conditioner. Measure the temperature on the inside and on the outside. Write your results in the table.
2. Go to a window that has an air conditioner. Measure the temperature on the inside and on the outside **right next to the air conditioner**. Write your results in the table.
3. If your building has an air conditioner unit completely outside, measure the temperature inside in any room and outside **right next to the air conditioner**. Write your results in the table.
4. Measure the temperature on the front outside of a refrigerator. Then open the refrigerator and measure the inside temperature. Then measure the temperature **behind the refrigerator**. Be careful if it is a full-sized refrigerator! Write your results in the table.

Location	Temperature inside (°F/°C)	Temperature outside (°F/°C)	Temperature other (°F/°C)
window, no AC			
window, AC			
inside/external AC			
refrigerator			

Can We Control Climate?

Questions:

1. Compare the inside temperatures to the outside temperatures. For which situation is the difference the largest?

2. Do any of the temperature results surprise you? Explain.

3. How does the outside temperature compare to the outside temperature near the air conditioner? Explain why there may be a difference, especially on cooler days.

4. Comment on the statement "We don't control climate, we just move it around."

5. Is it possible to use an air conditioner as a heater? If not, explain why. If so, explain why it may not be a good idea.

6. Based on your results, explain how a refrigerator works.

7. Could you cool a room by opening a refrigerator? Explain why or why not.

How Does a Greenhouse Work?

A greenhouse is a building made out of glass that keeps very warm inside. This allows plants to grow as they would outside in the summer. The green visible through the clear glass gives the building the name "greenhouse." How does a greenhouse stay warm without heaters? In this activity, you will find out by making your own (small) greenhouse.

Materials:

- scissors
- tape
- plastic wrap
- thermometer
- refrigerator
- black construction paper
- cardboard box at least 12" (30 cm) on each side

Method:

Follow the steps to construct the greenhouse shown in the picture. **Be careful with the scissors!**

1. Cut the top flaps off the box.
2. Tape the flaps together so they make a flat rectangle. This will be a removable roof.
3. Cut a window 1.5" x 1.5" (4 cm x 4 cm) near the bottom on one of the sides. Reattach the cut-out part as a flap using the tape.
4. Put black construction paper on the inside floor of the box.
5. You are now going to measure the temperature inside your greenhouse under three different conditions. After reading all the instructions, predict which set up will be warmest and which will be coolest. Record your results in the table.
6. With no cover on the box, put in the thermometer and record the temperature. Let it sit for three hours. Then record the new temperature.
7. Cover the box with the cardboard roof you made. Record the starting temperature inside the box by sliding the thermometer through the window. Then measure temperature again after three hours.
8. Remove the cardboard cover. Completely cover the top with plastic and tape it to the sides. Measure the inside temperature. Then measure the temperature after three hours.
9. If it is really cold outside, repeat the experiment out there. Otherwise, use a refrigerator.

How Does a Greenhouse Work?

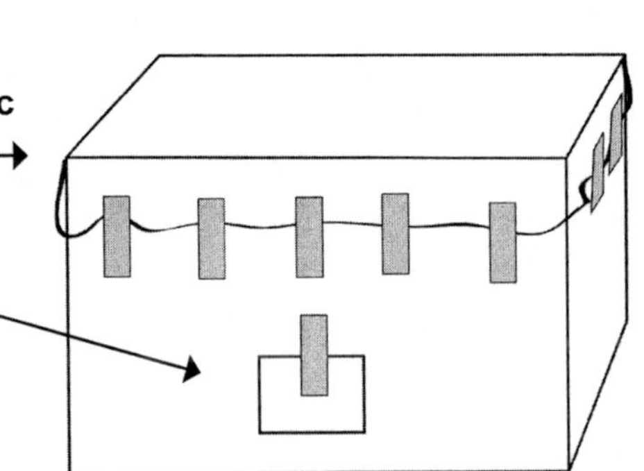

Results:

Prediction for warmest set up: ______________ Prediction for coldest set up: ______________

Set up	Starting Temperature (°F/°C)	Ending Temperature (°F/°C)
no cover		
roof		
plastic cover		
outside/fridge no cover		
outside/fridge roof		
outside/fridge plastic cover		

Questions:

1. Compare your results to your predictions. Were you correct? Do any of the results surprise you? Explain.______________________________

____

2. Compare the temperature differences from the normal room and in a colder environment. Which set up had the largest difference? Does this surprise you? Explain.

____

____

3. What do you think would happen to the temperature inside the box if you let it sit for a day? If you are not sure, try it and explain the results.

____

____

Clouds Over the Greenhouse

Do greenhouses work if it is cloudy outside? Do greenhouses work at night? Is the color of the glass important? Try these changes with the greenhouse you have just built.

Materials:
- greenhouse with plastic topping
- colored plastic wrap (black, red, blue, green, yellow, white, clear)
- aluminum foil

Method:

You are going to put different layers **on top** of your clear plastic-topped greenhouse. After reading all the instructions, predict which set up will be the coolest and which will be the warmest. For each set up, record the starting temperature and the temperature after three hours. The set ups are listed in the table where you can write in your results.

Prediction for coolest set up: _______________ Prediction for warmest set up: _____________

Results:

Set Up	Starting Temperature (°F/°C)	Temperature After 3 hours (°F/°C)
normal, one layer clear plastic		
three layers of clear plastic		
three layers of black plastic		
three layers of red plastic		
three layers of blue plastic		
three layers of green plastic		
three layers of yellow plastic		
three layers of white plastic		
one layer of aluminum foil		
half-covered by aluminum foil		
quarter-covered by aluminum foil		

Clouds Over the Greenhouse

Questions:

1. Compare the results to your predictions. Were you correct? Explain.

2. Based on your results, which color keeps a greenhouse warmest? Would this be a good choice to make a real greenhouse? Explain, remembering the purpose of a greenhouse.

3. Imagine you want to build a greenhouse with colored windows. One builder tells you that green is the best choice. Another builder says red is the best choice. A third builder says that clear is the best choice. Design an experiment to figure out who is correct. Again, remember the purpose of a greenhouse.

4. Explain how the pieces of aluminum foil over the greenhouse act like clouds.

5. What real life condition is created by completely covering the greenhouse with the foil? Explain.

6. Do greenhouses still work when it is cloudy? Are they better or worse? Explain.

7. Some areas near deserts have dusty air. Dust reflects a lot of light from the sun. Other areas like cities can be covered by smog. Smog also reflects a lot of light from the sun. How do you think the temperature in a greenhouse would be changed by dusty or smoggy skies? Design an experiment using your model greenhouse to find out.

Greenhouses are Traps

Greenhouses contain plants. Plants need air. So greenhouses cannot be air-tight. What are they trapping instead? In this experiment you will find out.

Materials:

- plastic wrap
- scissors
- tape
- thermometers
- seven plastic-covered greenhouse models

Method:

This experiment uses seven greenhouses to speed everything up. You can also use just one greenhouse, but it will take several days to complete the experiment. It is very important that the greenhouses have the same lighting conditions. Putting them all in one room with overhead lights and drawn curtains is one way of doing this. Having them all outside is another way.

You will cut holes into six of the greenhouses. **Be careful with the scissors!** The table lists all the seven set ups. To cut a hole, follow these general instructions:

1. Cut a hole on one side of the greenhouse to within 1" (2.5 cm) of each edge.
2. If directed, tape one layer of plastic over the hole, covering holes completely.

Before you begin, predict which set up will be warmest and which will be coolest.

Prediction for coolest set up:_______________ Prediction for warmest set up: _____________

Results:

Set Up	Starting Temperature (°F/°C)	Temperature after 3 hours (°F/°C)
normal, plastic top		
one hole in side		
two holes in sides		
three holes in sides		
one side hole plastic covered		
two side holes plastic covered		
three side holes plastic covered		

Greenhouses are Traps

Questions:

1. Compare the results to your predictions. Were you correct? Explain.

2. Compare the temperatures for the open holes compared to those with plastic over the holes. Is the temperature difference as large as you would have thought? Explain.

3. Holes let out air. Do your results agree with this statement? Is it possible for the statement to be right and your results to be right? Explain.

4. Explain why on a hot day it is possible to pass out underneath a bus shelter that is open to the air.

5. Climate change could result in some cities having thicker air sit over top of them. Pretending this air acts like plastic, explain what will happen to the city.

6. What kinds of cities will be best protected from the situation described above? (Hint: Think about wind patterns.)

Humidity Part A - What is Humidity?

Sometimes it feels hotter or colder than the air temperature. This is because of water vapor in the air, or humidity. People and animals find it hard to function if they are uncomfortable. Humidity can change this comfort level, especially if it is high and the air is warm. This activity will help you understand what humidity is.

Materials:

- thermometer
- lukewarm water
- 2 bowls
- measuring cup
- large plastic garbage bag
- humidifier or a source of steam (e.g., hot water tap in closed room, kettle)

Method:

1. Pour the lukewarm water into the bowl. Lukewarm means it is the same temperature as the air. Use the thermometer to confirm this.

2. Wet your hand in the lukewarm water. Remove your hand. Compared to your dry hand, your wet hand feels (warmer, cooler, or the same): ______________

3. Put the bowl of lukewarm water into the garbage bag. Fill the garbage bag with air from the humidifier. If you do not have a humidifier, put the bowl in a closed room with a hot water tap. Run the tap until it steams up a bit in the room.

4. Wet your hand in the water. Remove your hand, keeping it either inside the garbage bag or in the steamy room. Compared to your dry hand, your wet hand feels (warmer, cooler, or the same): ____

5. Pour 1 cup (250 mL) of water into each of two bowls. Put one bowl in the humidified garbage bag or steamy room and leave the other in a normal room. After one hour, measure the volume in the bowls. Which bowl has less water? ______________________________

Questions:

1. When water evaporates, does it take in heat or give it off? (Hint: How does a kettle work?) Explain. ____

____

____

____

Humidity Part A - What is Humidity?

2. Explain what happens to the water on your hand when you remove it from the bowl.

3. Explain the different volumes of water in the bowls in the humid and dry conditions.

4. Using your observations, and the answers to these questions, explain why you feel cold when you get out of a swimming pool.

5. Using your observations, and the answers to these questions, explain why you do not feel cold when you get out of a bath or shower in a steamy, closed room.

6. Climate change can affect temperature and humidity. Write down all the possible changes of wet, dry, hot, and cold. For example, hot and dry to hot and wet. Which one do you think would be the hardest to get used to? Which do you think would be the easiest to get used to?

7. "If there is a flood somewhere, there must be a drought somewhere else." Explain.

Humidity Part B - Measuring Humidity

The fact that a surface cools when water evaporates from it allows us to measure humidity. In this activity you will make a **hygrometer** to measure humidity. Then you can use it as you discover more about climate change.

Materials:

- two glass thermometers
- cotton batting (or torn up cotton balls)
- one nylon sock
- elastic bands
- a glass of water
- two plastic garbage bags
- kitty litter
- humidifier or steam source

Method:

1. Put a thin layer of kitty litter into one of the garbage bags and let it sit on the floor overnight.
2. Wrap the cotton around the bottom of one of the thermometers. Make sure not to cover up any of the lines above freezing (32°F/0°C).
3. Put the nylon over the cotton and stretch an elastic band over it to keep everything in place.
4. Put the cotton-wrapped thermometer in the glass of water and let it sit until the cotton is all wet.
5. Remove the wet thermometer from the water. Shake both it and the dry thermometer. Record the temperature of the wet thermometer as W and the dry thermometer as T.
6. Subtract T – W = D. This tells you how dry the air is.
7. Repeat steps 4-6 for any measurement of humidity. Try it in both the garbage bag with the kitty litter (dry) and a garbage bag that has been filled by a humidifier or steam (wet). Record your results below.

Location	**T** (temperature of dry thermometer)	**W** (temperature of wet thermometer)	**D = T – W**
room			
bag with kitty litter			
bag with steam			

Humidity Part B - Measuring Humidity

Questions:

1. Imagine two rooms at the same temperature. One room is humid while the other is dry. How will their **T** values compare? How will their **W** values compare? Explain.

2. Is it necessary to have a third thermometer to measure the room temperature? Explain.

3. How does the value of **D** compare to the dryness of the environment you measure? Explain.

4. What would happen to the accuracy of the hygrometer if the wet thermometer dried out?

5. When people use this kind of hygrometer outside, they usually swing it around in a circle on the end of a string for a few seconds. Explain why this is a good idea.

6. Some computer-based or "digital" thermometers measure humidity as well. They display it as a percentage, where 100% is full humidity. Write up a method for how you could use a computer thermometer to make a table of what your readings are in percentages. For this to work, the temperature will have to be the same.

Air in the Greenhouse

Have you ever walked inside a greenhouse? It probably felt really hot, like a sweaty summer day. Maybe you have visited a tropical exhibit at a zoo or museum. Why are these places so much hotter than the places outside? This activity will give you some answers.

Materials:

- plastic covered greenhouse
- hygrometer
- green plants (e.g., geraniums)
- humidifier
- sponge
- kitty litter
- glass of water
- pie plate
- paper towel or wrapping paper tube

Method:

In this experiment, you will have to use the hygrometer you have already made. Remember to keep the wet thermometer in the glass of water when you are not using it. The window you cut in the side of the greenhouse will allow you to slide the hygrometer in and out to take your readings.

You are going to create different types of air inside your plastic-topped greenhouse by putting different things **inside** your greenhouse:

1. normal – nothing inside
2. a plate of kitty litter
3. a wet sponge on the plate
4. a plant
5. humidify through the tube into a window for at least five minutes.

After reading all of the instructions, predict which set up will be the coolest and which will be the warmest. For each set up, record the starting temperatures and the temperatures after three hours. Remember that in the data table "W" is the temperature of the wet thermometer and "T" is the temperature of the dry thermometer. You are interested in the values of T and D = T – W.

Prediction for coolest set up: _______________ Prediction for warmest set up: _____________

Results:

Set Up	Start W (°F/°C)	Start T (°F/°C)	Start D (°F/°C)	W after 3 h (°F/°C)	T after 3 h (°F/°C)	D after 3 h (°F/°C)
normal						
kitty litter						
sponge						
plant						
humidified						

Air in the Greenhouse

Questions:

1. Compare your results to your predictions. Were you correct? Do any of the results surprise you? Explain. ______________________________

____

2 a) Using the D values for the measurements after three hours, list the set ups from **driest** to **wettest**. ______________________________

b) Using the T values for the measurements after three hours, list the set ups from **coldest** to **hottest**. ______________________________

c) Compare your two lists. What is the same? What is different?

____

____

3. How does wetter air affect temperature in a greenhouse? Explain.

____

____

4. Where does the wet air in a greenhouse come from? Suggest an experiment to see if your answer is correct. Pretend you have a real greenhouse to use in your experiment.

____

____

____

____

5. Why are rainforests so humid? Are all rainforests hot? Use classroom resources to find out.

____

____

Carbon Dioxide and Greenhouses

Humidity is good at keeping a greenhouse warm. But water vapor is not the only thing that can be in air. Carbon dioxide (CO_2) is a gas that is produced when things burn. This includes engines burning gasoline. When food digests in our bodies, it gets burned by our cells – like little engines. We breathe out the CO_2 because it is poisonous to us. Factories, animals, and cars also give off CO_2. What is the effect of CO_2 on a greenhouse?

Materials:

- three plastic covered greenhouses
- tape
- elastic bands
- kitty litter
- hygrometer
- vinegar
- baking soda
- tall drinking glasses
- measuring cup and measuring spoon

Method:

It is very important that the greenhouses have the same lighting conditions. Putting them all in one room with overhead lights and drawn curtains is one way of doing this. Having them all outside is another way.

Remember to predict the warmest and coolest set ups.

1. Sprinkle kitty litter onto the bottom of all three greenhouses.

2. In each of the other two greenhouses, place five drinking glasses inside. Pour 1 cup (250 mL) of vinegar into each drinking glass.

3. Cover the first two greenhouses with their plastic tops and tape shut. Stretch an elastic band around the plastic.

4. Tape one side of the plastic top on the third greenhouse. Have a friend hold the plastic back and another friend be ready with the elastic. Quickly drop 1 tbsp (15 mL) baking soda into each of the glasses of vinegar. Then quickly cover the top and seal it with tape and the elastic band.

5. Measure the starting temperature and humidity for all three greenhouses. Measure these values every 10 minutes for at least one hour. You can measure the temperature as long as you want.

Carbon Dioxide and Greenhouses

Prediction for coolest set up: ______________________

Prediction for warmest set up: ______________________

Results:

Normal Greenhouse

Time	T	W	D = T – W

Vinegar Greenhouse

Time	T	W	D = T – W

Vinegar + Baking Soda Greenhouse

Time	T	W	D = T – W

Graph the temperature of each of your greenhouses over time on the axes on the next page. Put all of the data on the same graph, using different colors or symbols to tell apart the different greenhouses.

Questions:

1. Look at your predictions and the results for the last measurement. Were you correct? Does anything surprise you? Explain.

____

____

____

Carbon Dioxide and Greenhouses

2. Looking at the graph you have made, which greenhouse had the warmest conditions? Did this trend continue? Comment on anything that catches your attention.

3. Vinegar burns baking soda in a way similar to how our cells burn up bread. Both processes release CO_2 and might release water vapor. What is the amount of CO_2 in each greenhouse compared to the other? What is the amount of water vapor in each greenhouse compared to the other? Explain how your results show this.

4. Since the Earth is like a greenhouse, why are people worried about how much CO_2 is in the atmosphere?

A Natural Greenhouse

Look at a picture of the Earth from space. It has green on parts of the continents – forests. But space is really cold. How does Earth keep warm enough to grow plants?

http://nssdc.gsfc.nasa.gov/planetary/image/earth_day.jpg

1. Look over what you have learned from making your own greenhouse and experimenting with it. Write down what is needed to make a greenhouse.

2. What properties of air can make a greenhouse warmer?

3. Thinking of the oceans, land, plants, sky, and sun, explain why Earth can be thought of as a greenhouse.

4. Draw a picture of the Earth as a greenhouse. Be sure to label your drawing so others can understand your thinking.

The Color of Earth

Look at a picture of the Earth at
http://nssdc.gsfc.nasa.gov/planetary/image/earth_day.jpg.

List the colors you can see: ______________________________

How do these colors affect how hot the Earth gets? You can find out by trying on some clothes.

Materials:

- ✪ blankets/sheets of white, green, brown, dark blue
- ✪ desk lamp or sunlight

Method:

You will put on one of the blankets for five minutes. You will rate on a scale of 1 to 10 how warm you feel. A "1" is how you feel with no blanket, a "10" is overheated.

Color	Prediction	Rating
white		
green		
brown		
blue		

Questions:

1. Compare your results to your predictions. Were you right? Does anything surprise you? Explain. ______________________________

   ____

2. Why do people in hot, sunny climates wear lots of white?

   ____

   ____

3. Compare Antarctica to one of the oceans. Which one will get hotter under a lot of sun? Explain. ______________________________

   ____

4. Compare northern Africa to northern South America. Which will be hotter at night? Explain.

   ____

   ____

   ____

Will the Earth Heat Evenly?

Look at a map of a cloudless Earth from space at
http://nssdc.gsfc.nasa.gov/planetary/image/earth_day.jpg

1. Can you figure out which places are the hottest? (Hint: Think about how warm or cold you feel in differently colored clothing.) On the map below, circle where you think it will be the hottest.

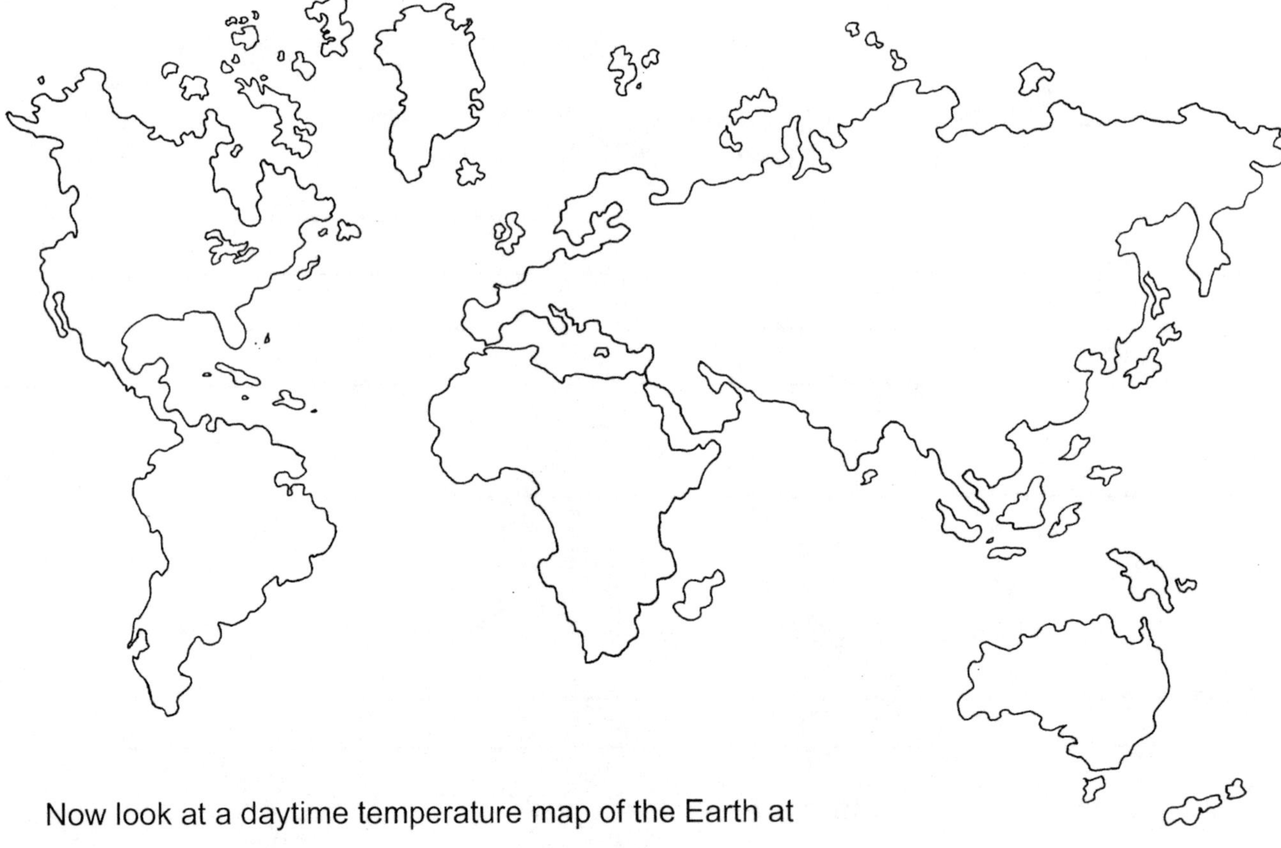

Now look at a daytime temperature map of the Earth at

http://neo.sci.gsfc.nasa.gov/Search.html?group=19

2. How correct are your predictions? Explain any differences.

____

____

____

3. Compare Greenland to northern Canada and Russia. Why is Greenland colder?

____

____

Will the Earth Heat Evenly?

4. Look at northern Africa and northern South America. Which is hotter? Does this surprise you? Explain. ____
____
____

5. Look at the temperature of the oceans.

   http://veimages.gsfc.nasa.gov/2366/sst_lar.jpg

   Explain the map. (Hint: what color are oceans?)
   ____
   ____
   ____

6. Now look at a **nighttime** temperature map of the Earth at

   http://neo.sci.gsfc.nasa.gov/Search.html?group=51

   Look again at northern Africa and northern South America. What happened? Explain why.
   ____
   ____
   ____

7. Explain the temperature changes experienced by a hot desert over a 24 hour period.
   ____
   ____
   ____

8. Looking at the Earth, imagine the air getting hotter. Will every part of the Earth heat evenly? In a different color, circle regions that you think will get hotter. Explain your reasoning.
   ____
   ____
   ____
   ____

9. What changes may people living in the circled regions need to make? Will people living outside of the circled regions need to change? Explain.
   ____
   ____
   ____

Water and Ice and Heat

The Arctic is an ocean covered with ice. There is no solid land underneath, unlike in Antarctica. In the summer, the sun shines for 24 hours on the Arctic, so some of the ice melts. Global warming is making the ice melt faster. This activity will help you figure out why this has many people really worried about the Arctic.

1. a) Think about what you have learned about color and temperature. (Hint: Would you rather have a dark or a light coat in the winter?) Circle the picture that is the warmest:

ice floes

open ocean

ice with holes

   b) Explain your decision.

   ____

   ____

2. In the pictures above, the left shows Arctic ice at the end of a warm summer and the right shows it at the end of a cold summer. When the sun goes away in the autumn, the ice begins to freeze again. Look at these overhead maps of the Arctic. Circle the picture that shows what the ice looks like after six months of freezing after a cold summer? What about after a warm summer?

ice floes

solid ice

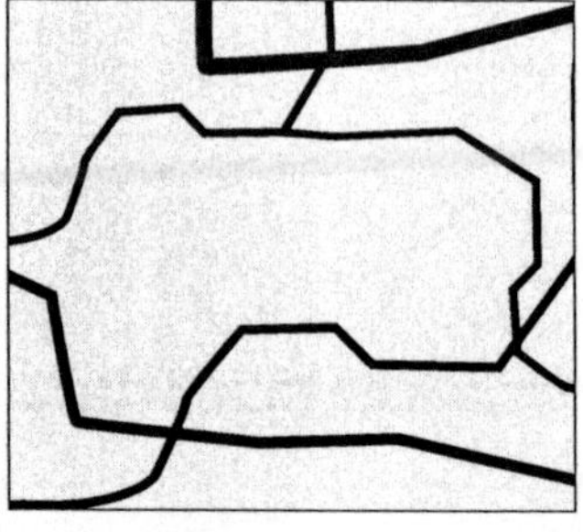

cracked ice

holes in ice

Water and Ice and Heat

3. a) Imagine that one summer ALL of the ice melts. Draw the end of summer and beginning of the following summer.

end of summer | **beginning of next summer**

b) Now imagine that the next year all of the ice melts by halfway through the summer. Draw what it will look like at the end of summer and at the beginning of the next summer.

end of summer | **beginning of next summer**

c) Explain your drawings above.

4. If the summer picture you predict becomes normal, what will happen to the temperature of the Arctic? Explain.

Water and Ice and Heat

5. Explain why global warming will first be experienced in the Arctic.

____

____

____

Feedback

Dark land heats up. White land cools down. Is it possible to have dark land turn into white land? What effect would this have on climate?

Imagine a forest in the north. The trees surround a lake. Here is an overhead picture of this:

A

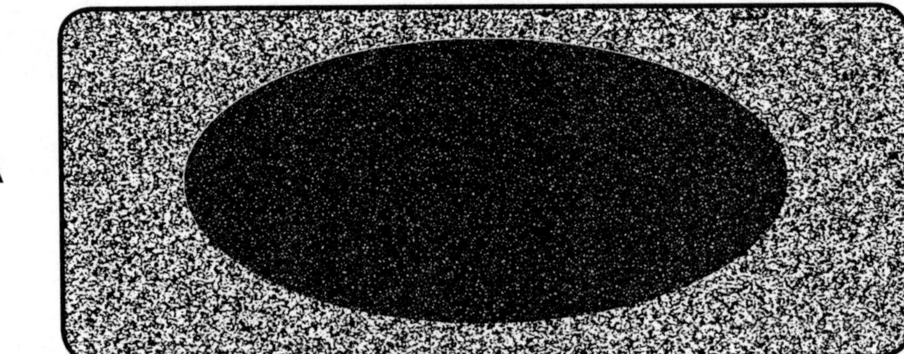

1. a) The lake water evaporates as it warms and makes a cloud. Draw an overhead picture of this:

B

b) Compare picture A to picture B. Which is warmer? Explain.

____

____

____

Water and Ice and Heat

2. a) Imagine picture B takes place in the winter, so the cloud drops snow. Draw the overhead scene after the snowfall stops. (Assume the clouds go away.)

C

b) Compared to picture A, is picture C hotter, colder, or the same? Explain.

____

____

3. Imagine that it snows again and the lake freezes. Then it snows again. Draw the overhead scene.

D

4. a) Draw a graph showing the temperature trend from picture A to B to C to D. Remember to label your graph.

b) Explain how the temperature kept changing from picture A to picture D.

____

____

Water and Ice and Heat

Questions:

5. In nature sometimes things change in such a way that it makes the next change faster. But only if the change is in the same direction. This is called **feedback**. Explain why the overhead scenes you have drawn are an example of feedback.

____

____

____

6. Imagine that the normal temperature for picture B is 30°F (-1°C). Imagine that global warming causes the picture to be at 32°F (0°C). Draw a new temperature graph and explain it compared to the original.

____

____

____

____

Water and Ice and Heat

7. Imagine that global warming raises the temperature in picture B to 35°F (2°C). Draw a new temperature graph and explain it compared to the original.

8. Feedback can also cause warming. Explain why global warming with more days above freezing could cause Arctic ground to thaw. Should that ground still be called "permafrost"?

9. Explain why even a few degrees temperature change can cause huge changes in climate.

Moving Water in the Oceans

Have you ever seen a hot air balloon? When its fire is on, the balloon rises. When its fire is out, the balloon sinks. This is because hot air rises and cold air sinks. Air is a fluid because it flows to fill its container. Water is a fluid for the same reason. So like air, hot water rises and cold water sinks. Try this activity to see if this is true.

Materials:

- heat resistant glass bowl or pot (coffee pot ideal)
- water
- hot plate
- small pasta shells or rice

Method:

1. Under the supervision of your teacher, fill the pot and set it on the hot plate to boil.
2. When the water starts bubbling, add a **few** pasta shells or rice.
3. Draw the path these shells or rice take in the water. Show their direction with arrows:

In the ocean, warm water forms along the equator. Water at the poles is very cold because it does not get as much sun, even in the summer. This polar water sinks and runs along the ocean bottom. This pushes the warm water to where the cold used to be. Now the warm water gets cold. Explain why this diagram shows water moving in the Atlantic Ocean: (the top of the ocean is at the top of the picture)

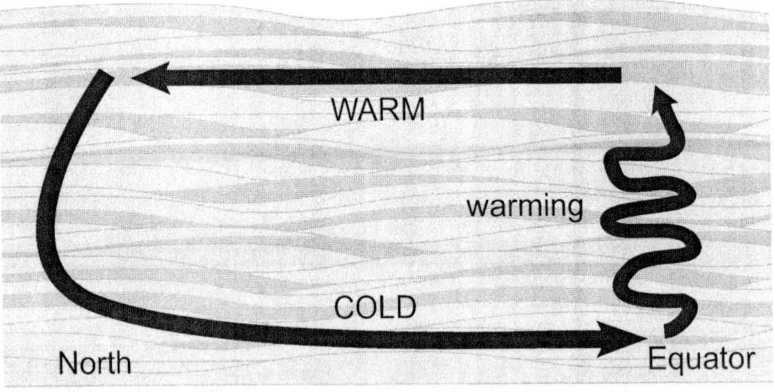

Ocean Circulation

Using boats, submarines, robots, and satellites, scientists have mapped where water goes in the ocean: **http://scienceblogs.com/deepseanews/2007/08/post_6.php**

Read about this map at **http://oceanservice.noaa.gov/education/kits/currents/06conveyor.html** and watch **http://svs.gsfc.nasa.gov/vis/a010000/a010000/a010031/oceanconvey.mpg** Discuss these as a class with your teacher. Then answer the questions.

Questions:

1. Why do you think the paths are not simple straight lines?

____

____

2. Circle regions on the map where the arrows curl back on themselves. What is happening at these regions?

____

____

____

3. Look at the Davis Strait between Greenland and Québec. Scientists sometimes call this a "dive zone." Explain why.

____

____

____

4. Imagine you are a water molecule starting in the Caribbean. Draw the path you will take.

5. Scientists have calculated that it takes 500 – 1000 years to make the journey you just tracked. Does this surprise you? Explain.

____

____

____

6. The circulation path of water is nicknamed the "ocean conveyor". Using your understanding of how conveyor belts work in a factory (or cafeteria), explain why this is a good nickname.

____

____

____

Changing the Current

As global warming changes the Arctic, the effect could change a large part of the world. This model will show you how the weather may change if Arctic and Greenland ice melts fast.

Materials:

- several red and blue marbles
- a square of carpet – about 4.5 sq ft (0.5 m^2)
- paper
- scissors
- roll of masking tape

Method:

Read all these instructions carefully before starting the simulation. Note there is a question to answer part way through the instructions.

1. Cut the paper to look like the Gulf of Mexico, Cuba, the Eastern Seaboard of the USA and Canada (Florida to Newfoundland), Greenland, Iceland, Ireland, England and the coast of western Europe. Assemble these properly on the square of carpet. Label the land masses.

2. Place the masking tape ring on Greenland.

3. Form two teams – Team Blue and Team Red. Every five seconds, Team Blue will drop a marble on the north part of the map. Every 5 seconds, Team Red will roll a red marble from Florida to England. Continue until the masking tape ring is almost full.

4. Answer this question: If blue marbles represent cold water and ice and red marbles represent warm water, explain why Greenland is colder than England.

   ____

   ____

5. Now you will simulate global warming. Team Blue will continue on as before. Team Red will continue as before, but also drop a red marble on the north every 10 seconds.

6. When 10 red marbles end up in the masking tape ring, lift away the ring quickly to let the marbles spill out. Team Blue and Team Red should continue. Watch carefully and answer the questions.

Changing the Current

Questions:

1. What does the masking tape ring represent?

2. What does the removal of the masking tape ring represent? Why does it happen?

3. What happens to the number of red marbles that England gets **after** the masking tape ring is removed? What will this cause?

4. Explain how the removal of the masking tape ring might change:

   a) the weather in Maine

   b) the weather in Spain

   c) the weather in Florida.

5. Explain why global warming may cause "climate change", and not necessarily "climate warming". Discuss your answers with the class.

6. In the movies, the change you have simulated has been shown to happen in a few days. Explain why this is impossible, but that the change could happen in a matter of years.

Rising Seas and Shores

One of the biggest worries about global warming is that snow and ice will melt into the ocean. This will raise the sea level anywhere from 0 to 20 ft (0 to 6.1 m). But the oceans are HUGE! Why are people so worried about coastal cities? This experiment will help you see.

Materials:

- plastic cutting board
- Plasticine
- water
- ruler
- 9" x 13" (23 x 33 cm) baking pan, preferably glass

Method:

1. Lay the cutting board in the pan as shown, using Plasticine to secure it.

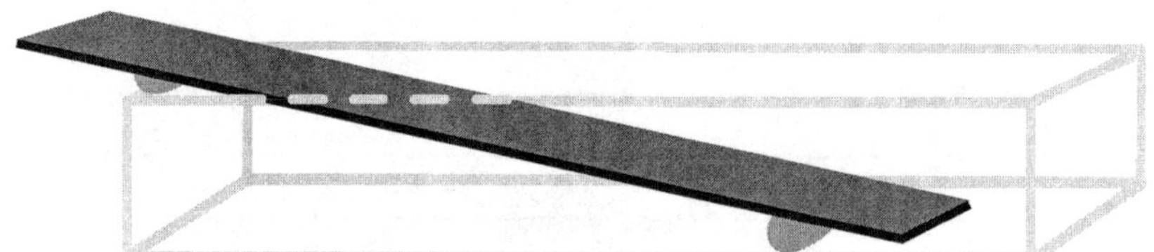

2. Add water to the pan so it just touches the end of the board. Measure this depth and record it in the table.
3. Add 0.5" (1.3 cm) of water to the pan. With a piece of Plasticine, mark where the water on the board comes up.
4. Repeat Step 3 until the pan is full.
5. Remove the board being **careful to keep the Plasticine marks in place**. Measure how far they are from the starting point and record the data in the Table. Then calculate the **area** of the board that was covered by each increase of 0.5" (1.3 cm) of water. Add that data to the table.

Results:

Water Depth (in/cm)	**Distance from End of Board** (in/cm)	**Area Covered** (sq in/cm^2)

Rising Seas and Shores

Questions:

1. Compare the change of water depth to how much of the board was covered. Explain the difference. (Hint: Compare depth to area.)

____

____

2. Imagine that the pan is the ocean and the board is the land, with its coast. Another name for the water depth is sea level. Explain this naming.

____

____

3. Imagine that in this model of ocean and land, 0.5" (1.3 cm) represents 5' (1.5 m). Calculate how far inland and what land area is covered using these numbers.

Distance Inland (0.5" = 5'; 1.3 cm = 1.5 m)	Area Covered (sq ft/m^2)

4. Look at pictures of a coastal city. What do you notice about the height of the streets compared to the ocean? Why are people that live in these cities and others like them worried about sea level rising up to 20 ft (6.1 m)?

____

____

____

____

____

5. Look at this web site and experiment with different sea level changes: **http://geongrid.geo.arizona.edu/arcims/website/slrworld/viewer.htm** Why are people so worried that sea level could increase up to 20 ft (6.1 m)? What will happen to people in coastal cities?

____

____

____

____

Icebergs and Sea Level

The Arctic and Antarctic are covered with ice. Every year in the summer, some of this ice cracks and some of it melts. Global warming is causing this to happen more. This means more icebergs are going to enter the ocean. So which is worse? Ice melting or more icebergs? Try this to find out.

Materials:
- ice cubes
- 2 identical glasses
- water
- ruler

Method:

1. In one glass, put in one ice cube. In the other glass, put in as many ice cubes as you can, even stacking them above the rim.

2. Fill both glasses to the brim. Predict what will happen when the ice melts:

Glass 1 ______________________ Glass 2 ___________________________

3. Let the ice melt. Write what happened below:

Glass 1 ______________________ Glass 2 ___________________________

Questions:

1. Were your predictions correct? Did any results surprise you? Explain.

____

____

2. What happens if a glass of water filled to the brim has an ice cube added to it?

____

3. Which will raise sea level more: icebergs already in the ocean melting or new icebergs being added to the ocean? Explain.

____

____

____

____

Glaciers and Sea Level

The source of ice in the ocean is ice pack floating in the water and glaciers on land pushing in new ice. The Arctic Ocean is an example of ice pack; Greenland and Antarctica are examples of glaciers. Global warming is causing more ice to melt. Which type of melting ice is worse for sea level: ice pack or glaciers? Try this experiment to find out.

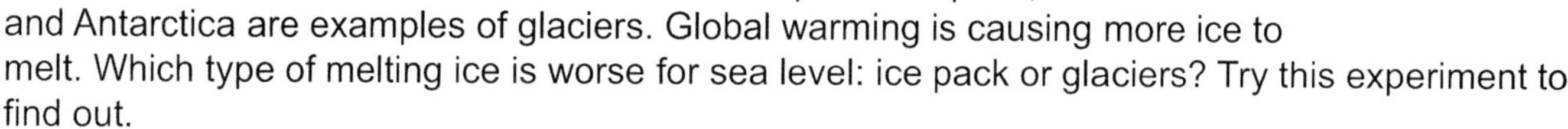

Materials:

- 9" x 13" (23 x 33 cm) pan
- cutting board
- Plasticine
- water
- ruler
- ice cubes
- salt and measuring spoon

Method:

1. Set up the cutting board in the pan using Plasticine as shown in the picture:

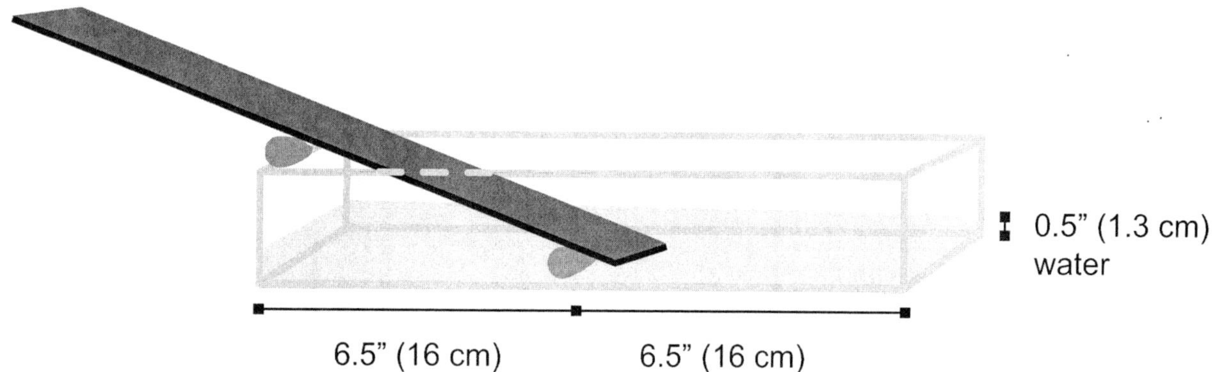

2. Add 1 tbsp (15 mL) of salt to the water and stir it with your hand.
3. When the water comes to a rest, fill the water with ice cubes and completely cover the board with them. **Some of the ice cubes will be completely out of the water.**
4. Measure the starting water depth and record the number in the table. Continue to record the water depth every 10 minutes. Whenever an ice cube slides into the water, measure the depth.
5. When all the ice has melted, graph your data on the axes. Remember to label your graph.

Glaciers and Sea Level

Results:

Time	Water Depth (in/cm)

Glaciers and Sea Level

Questions:

1. What happens to the water level over time? Does this surprise you? Explain.

2. Circle part of your graph where the biggest change in water level occurred. Compare this amount of change to what happened at the start. Why is there a difference?

3. What increases water depth more: an ice cube in the water melting or new ice cubes entering the water? Explain.

4. Look at the two pictures below.

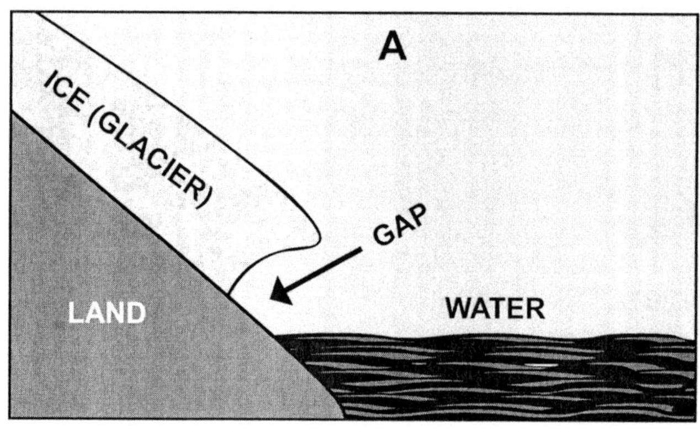

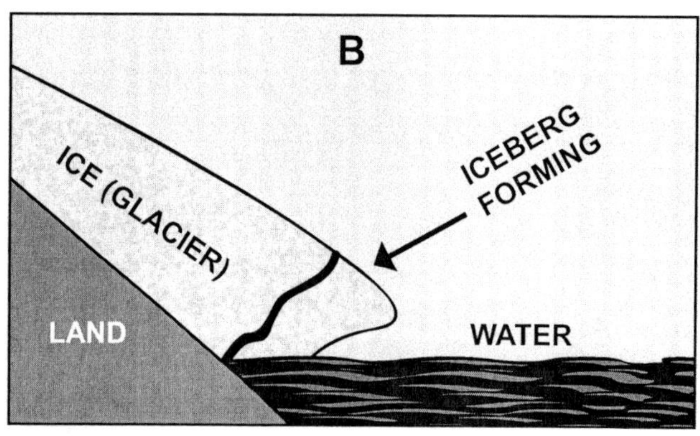

As temperatures rise, which picture will result in a larger increase in sea level? Explain.

5. Watch *An Inconvenient Truth* from time 54:18 to 1:01:10. Explain how this experiment demonstrates what the film predicts.

Relative Impact

The amount of change a system can handle depends on its starting point. Some systems can handle more change than others.

See how adding ice cubes to different water systems change their temperatures.

Materials:

- ice cubes
- chilled water (from a refrigerator)
- water at room temperature
- hot water from a tap
- drinking glass
- bucket
- thermometer

Procedure:

Follow these steps for each of the samples listed below. All numbers are to be recorded in the table on the next page.

1. Measure the starting temperature of the water.

2. Add one ice cube to the water. Measure the temperature after five minutes.

3. With a new sample of the same kind, repeat steps 1 and 2 with five ice cubes.

Samples:

- chilled water in a drinking glass
- chilled water in a bucket
- room temperature water in a drinking glass
- room temperature water in a bucket
- hot water in a drinking glass
- hot water in a bucket

Hypothesis:

Predict which sample will experience the greatest change:______________________________

Predict which sample will experience the least change:________________________________

Relative Impact

Results:

Sample	Starting Temperature		Temperature After 5 minutes	
	1 cube	5 cubes	1 cube	5 cubes
chilled in glass				
chilled in bucket				
room T. in glass				
room T. in bucket				
hot in glass				
hot in bucket				

Questions:

1. Check your hypothesis and your results. Were you correct?

____

2. Which sample had the largest temperature change? Which sample had the smallest temperature change? Does this make sense? Explain.

____

____

____

3. Predict what would happen to each sample if you added boiling water instead of ice cubes.

____

____

4. The July high for Boise, ID, is 89°F (32°C). The July high for Milwaukee, WI, is 81°F (27°C). Both cities have a latitude of 43°N. Milwaukee is on the coast of Lake Michigan and Boise is not near any lakes.

   a) Explain why Boise is warmer than Milwaukee.

____

____

____

   b) If the climate were to suddenly change, would Boise or Milwaukee feel it first? Which city may have more problems in the long run?

____

____

____

Local Affects Global

An obstacle course is a race that takes extra time because you cannot run straight through. Sometimes an obstacle that seems short by itself can cause really long delays. The local obstacle affects the global race time. Run and change this obstacle course with your class to see how local affects global.

The Method:

1. Three people are needed as Controllers for the obstacle course.
2. Divide the rest of the class into three teams (A, B, and C). Each team will run the obstacle course a total of three times. Teams not racing record the race time.
3. The course has three stations, or obstacles. Controllers allow racers to go once they have passed the station.

Station 1 – Spell a word backwards from either List A or List B. The Controller will read through the list in order and repeat from the top if the team has more than 10 people.

List A: rain, snow, wind, sun, cloud, sky, water, hot, cold, ice

List B: meteorology, climatology, temperature, greenhouse, glacier, hurricane, tornado, erosion, atmosphere, prediction

Station 2 – Each person must wait a set time before passing through.

Station 3 – List favorite things according to the time showing on the clock

0 – 19 seconds	favorite days of the week
20 – 39 seconds	favorite foods
40 – 59 seconds	favorite books

4. On the next page, Table 1 lists how each station's rules change for each run. There is space to fill in the time each team takes. Then divide the time by the number of people on the team.
5. After Run 6, you and your class will come up with three new rules to try and speed up the race. Write these rules in Table 2 and fill in the times (total and time per person).
6. Answer the questions.

Local Affects Global

Race 1

Run	Team	Station 1 Rule	Station 2 Rule	Station 3 Rule	Total Time (min:sec)	Time/Number of People
1	A	List A	3 s wait	list 3 things		
2	B	List A	3 s wait	list 3 things		
3	C	List A	3 s wait	list 3 things		
4	A	List B	3 s wait	list 3 things		
5	B	List A	5 s wait	list 3 things		
6	C	List A	3 s wait	list 5 things		

Based on the Times for Runs 1-6, make up a different rule for Station 1, Station 2, and Station 3 to **speed up the race**. **The new rule cannot remove the Station.** Fill out Table 2.

Race 2

Run	Team	Station 1 Rule	Station 2 Rule	Station 3 Rule	Total Time (min:sec)	Time/Number of People
7	A		3 s wait	list 3 things		
8	B	List A		list 3 things		
9	C	List A	3 s wait			

Questions:

1. Look at the times for Runs 1-3. The times per number of people are probably different. What reasons could explain this? ______________________________

____

2. Look at the times for Runs 4-6 and 7-9. Which station rule change made the biggest time difference? Which rule change made the least time difference? Explain why a local obstacle change affects the global race. ______________________________

____

____

3. "The local changes the global." Explain why everyone is responsible for climate change.

____

____

____

Natural and Artificial

Natural things happen by themselves. Artificial things happen because of people.

Write whether each is "natural' or "artificial" or both.

- cold air makes it snow ____________________
- freezers make snow ____________________
- clouds form over warm water ____________________
- clouds can form in a steamy bathroom ____________________
- fluorescent lights can help plants grow ____________________
- plants grow in greenhouses ____________________
- the Earth is like a greenhouse ____________________

Compare your answers with a partner. Do you agree? If yes, think of how one of the statements could be natural or artificial. Try to convince each other of the opposite choice.

Discuss the reasons with your partner and report to the class.

Questions:

1. In your own words, define artificial using an example.

____

____

2. In your own words, define natural using an example.

____

____

3. "There is a strong breeze next to the road." Explain how this statement could be natural or artificial. ____________________

____

____

4. Using your own knowledge and classroom resources, explain how climate change can be natural or artificial.

____

____

____

____

Sources and Sinks

Many substances "cycle" through nature. A cycle means that these substances collect in one place and are released from another. It is important to understand these cycles to understand nature. Once you understand nature then you can better figure out how climate may change.

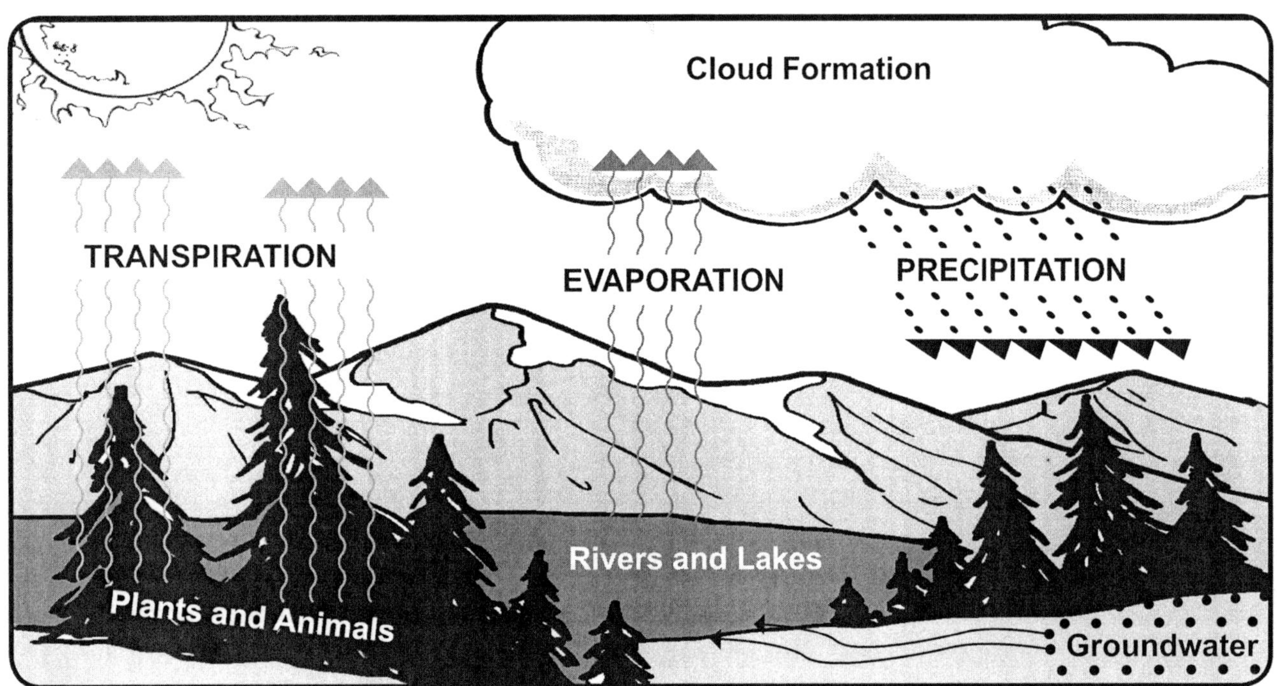

In the water cycle shown in the picture, a source is where water enters the cycle, such as evaporation. A sink is where water is held for a time, such as in a lake or in soil. Some parts of the cycle are both sources and sinks. Plants and animals take in water to grow (sink) then give it off as waste (source).

The carbon dioxide (CO_2) cycle is also made up of sources and sinks. Some of these are listed below, and some are actually both a source and a sink. Your teacher will assign you to groups and each group will get one or more of these locations. Using your own knowledge and classroom resources, find out if your locations are a source, a sink, or both. Report back to the class, and then answer the questions that follow.

- forests
- oceans
- volcanoes
- factories
- cars
- animals and people
- limestone rocks

Sources and Sinks

Questions:

1. CO_2 warms the air. What sources of CO_2 are the biggest concerns for global warming? Explain. ______

2. Climate change has occurred in the past, before there were people and factories on Earth. When the Earth's crust was young, explain why there was more CO_2 in the air. Can you think of the sink that pulled in enough CO_2 to make Earth cooler like it is today?

3. Suggest a way of decreasing the amount of CO_2 in the air using natural sources and sinks.

4. Suggest a way of decreasing the amount of CO_2 in the air using artificial sources and sinks.

5. Between using natural versus artificial sources and sinks to decrease the amount of CO_2 in the air, which methods do you think are faster? Easier? Less expensive? Better? Discuss your reasons together in your group and report back to the class.

Debating Pollution

Both water vapor and carbon dioxide (CO_2) can cause global warming. Does that mean that all sources of water vapor and CO_2 are sources of pollution? In this activity, you will develop your own answer to that question, and then debate it with your classmates.

1. Think of the definitions of sources and sinks and natural and artificial. Now define pollution.

____

____

2. Water vapor released to the air causes warming. Explain which of the following are sources of pollution.

   a) bodies of water (lakes, rivers, oceans)

   ____

   ____

   b) swimming pools

   ____

   ____

   c) car exhaust

   ____

   ____

3. CO_2 released to the air causes warming. Explain which of the following are sources of pollution. Think deeply about forest fires – does it depend how they started?

   a) erupting volcanoes

   ____

   ____

   b) factories

   ____

   ____

   c) forest fires

   ____

   ____

Debating Pollution

4. Trees inhale CO_2. Forests are dark and soak up a lot of sunlight. Trees give off water vapor. Rain forests produce lots of clouds. Clouds reflect a lot of sunlight. Burning releases CO_2.

a) How can forests add to global **warming**?

____

____

b) How can forests add to global **cooling**?

____

____

5. What is your opinion of the phrase "natural pollution"?

____

____

Pollution Debate

The class will now divide into two groups. One side will argue in favor of the below statement, the other will argue against it. After the debate, answer the questions below.

Trees pollute.

Questions:

6. Before the debate, what was your opinion of the debating topic **regardless of which side you argued for**?

____

____

7. After the debate, has your opinion changed? Explain.

____

____

8. What are some questions that the debate raised in your mind?

____

____

9. Do you think it is important to have debates like this one? Explain.

____

____

An Inconvenient Truth Graphing

When detectives need to figure out what has happened, they look at evidence. Sometimes they need to look at very old evidence that helped previous detectives solve a different problem. Then it becomes easier to figure out what the present evidence is saying.

The connection between carbon dioxide (CO_2) and global warming has been made in several ways. One of the most convincing comes from what we know about past CO_2 levels and the temperature of the Earth.

In this activity, you will watch parts of the film *An Inconvenient Truth* and answer the questions below.

First, watch from the beginning to time index 11:50. Now pay careful attention until 22:43.

Questions:

1. What reasons were given for the annual CO_2 amounts going up and down?

____

____

2. In the past, when CO_2 levels went up, what happened to the Earth's temperature? When CO_2 levels went down, what happened to Earth's temperature?

____

____

3. How strong is the argument that Earth's temperature is affected by CO_2 levels? Explain.

____

____

____

Now watch from 22:43 to 24:35.

4. What do you expect to happen to Earth's temperature? What evidence do you have to support your answer?

____

____

5. What would be direct evidence that CO_2 causes global warming? Does this evidence exist?

____

____

____

Are Clouds Good or Bad?

Clouds form over water when the water warms up. How will global warming affect cloud formation? Will the result be good or bad?

1. When you walk under a cloud, do you feel hotter or colder? Why?

   ____

   ____

2. If it gets increasingly hot, what do you think will happen to the number of clouds?

   ____

   ____

3. If these clouds are over land, what will happen to the temperature of the land underneath? What if they are over water? Explain.

   ____

   ____

   ____

4. Open water is not the only source of vapor to make clouds. Hot air can also pull moisture out of soil. Explain why global warming could cause both floods and droughts.

   ____

   ____

   ____

   ____

5. Are clouds good or bad for global warming? Explain. Discuss your answer with the class.

   ____

   ____

   ____

http://earthobservatory.nasa.gov/GlobalMaps/view.php?d1=MODAL2_M_CLD_FR

Cities and Climate

Cities contain all kinds of sources and sinks that interact with the environment and affect climate change. It is important to understand all of these so that climate change can be tracked and its effects kept in check. In this activity, you will first think about how cities cause climate change. Then you will come up with ideas for cities to deal with climate change.

1. List sources of carbon dioxide found in cities.

2. List sources of water vapor found in cities.

3. List sinks for carbon dioxide found in cities.

4. List sinks for water vapor founds in cities.

5. Given your knowledge of global warming, how much are cities to blame?

6. What could be done within a city to decrease the amount of carbon dioxide produced?

7. What could be done in a city to keep water vapor levels in the atmosphere more constant?

8. How should coastal cities prepare for global warming? Is it a good idea to do this even if the sea level changes are not as serious as some predict? Explain.

Cities and Climates

9. A new building in Switzerland has been covered with metal fins that open or close to shade the building's many windows. Think about the greenhouse effect, sunlight reflection, and "dressing for the weather". Explain why this new building's climate control system does not require any heaters or air conditioners.

____

____

____

10. Buildings like the one described above are more expensive to build right now because they are new. What is an argument that more cities should build them anyway?

____

____

____

11. In the space below, do one of the following:

a) Draw a picture of a city that has made changes to slow or stop climate change. Label the picture and explain your choices to the class.

b) Write a letter to your mayor on how your community could be changed to slow or stop climate change. After your teacher checks it over, type it up and send it!

Answer Key

What is Weather? (page 14)

1. Answers may vary.
2. If it does not agree, it should say where the newspaper/Internet differed.

Climates of the World (page 15)

1. a) no coat (unless in southern hemisphere and/or rainy summer)
   b) yes coat (unless in southern hemisphere)
   c) July is summer, hot, no coat. January is winter, cold, coat. (inverse if Southern hemisphere)
2. a) loose clothing, hats, sandals, shorts, T-shirt/short-sleeves, tank top, dress/skirt, kaftan, etc.
   b) coat, leggings, socks, scarf, gloves/mitts, hat, earmuffs, sweater, boots, shawl, etc.
   c) raincoat, hat, umbrella, boots, poncho, etc.
   d) loose fitting clothing (hot), long sleeves/pants (cold), sandals, boots, hat, scarf (cold), etc.
   e) hat, sunglasses, umbrella/parasol, sunscreen, etc.
   f) coat, windbreaker, gloves/mitts, insulated clothing, etc.
3. Different ways to prepare: travel guides, newspaper reports, internet, books, talk to people from there or who have visited there. ect.
4. and 5. Depend on answers – should be on par with appropriate choices in question 2.
6. No, it could rain in the summer; sometimes strangely cold. Could also be warm in winter!
7. Internet, look up previously actual weather for that time of year; almanac, talk to people from there or who have visited there a lot, ect.

Weather or Climate? (page 17)

In order of listing:

W, W, C, C, W, C, C, W, C, WC, W, W, C, WC, W, C, C, C, C, W, C, C, WC, WC, C, W, W, C, W

1. Weather is specific, day-to-day, short time period. Climate is general AVERAGE, no specific temperatures or other measurements/conditions.
2. Along the lines of sunbathing in summer versus shoveling snow/cowering in winter cold.
3. Cold may have been in winter, hot in summer; deserts very hot during day but very cold (even freezing) at night; Morocco is mountainous and would be cold at elevation, especially at night.
4. Sudden climate change; climate is an average, over years; weather can change fast, in minutes or seconds sometimes (cloudburst), so quick weather change is expected.

Weather Patterns Make Climates (page 19)

1. If bars are tall, wet; if bars are short, dry.
2. It may have been wetter or drier than usual. Advanced reasoning: this graph only measures weather.
3. Same as question 1.
4. Yes, because the normal averaged out . . . unless it has been a strange month!
6. If numbers are always large, wet; if numbers are always small, dry.
7. Yes, 30 years is a long enough time for weird years to average out; but it is possible the month in question is wetter/drier than rest of year.

Measuring Change (page 23)

FAST – minutes or less; MEDIUM – hours; SLOW – days or more

Questions:

1. Hot water – room temperature; plant – stopped moving for a few days in a row; bread stopped changing color/decomposing; pavement – night fell; cloth – completely dry; dust – unending.
2. If something is watched long enough, it is possible to detect a difference. However, some things may take years to change so over a short time it looks like there is no change.
3. Narrow candle got shorter.
4. Volume of wax melted.
5. *Discuss with the class*; measure/observe different things (e.g., volume of wax with candle); one person may have seen the system before and knows what to look for; another person, being new, may notice change that another has stopped seeing.

Ideas of Change (page 25)

1. Older probably – seen more in their life; possibly middle group more observant to change.
2. 22-50 probably – depends on person's life experience(s).
3. Older seen most change, younger probably little or no change.
4. 22-50/older – more sensitive to changes.

Short Term and Long Term Change (page 28)

1. Overall change has more days so it evens out all the day-to-day changes.
2. Short term is less time, long term shows big picture (speak to "big picture" in discussions).
3. Looking at the short term, the change seems to be up and down/all over the place; trend line shows the overall/big picture change which is the 'real' change.

Temperature Trends (page 31)

1. No change is flat; big change - steep slope; warmer - slope upwards to right; cooler- slope downwards to right.
2. Weather is day-to-day change in temperature, rain, etc.; climate is the average of "weathers".
3. Week long – weather, short term; 20 years – climate, average (but can change as well).
4. No, not enough information/data OR yes, now much different than 20 years ago (axes' range).
5. Not changing – flat; no, cannot tell – all over the place; yes – definite increase or decrease.
6. In calculating an average it is better to have as many pieces of information as possible; seeing change in the average requires lots of data (discussion on "change in the change" nuance).
7. a) Colder than average, not normal; advanced reasoning will see diamond is same as weather about 10 years prior.
   b) Yes, there is an upward trend.
   c) Yes, the trend is still upwards, just not as much.

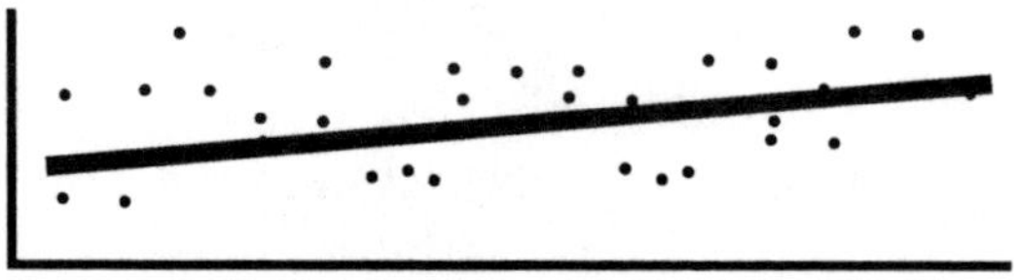

Watering Changes (page 34)

2. Probably the extremes; control (normal for six weeks) probably healthiest.
3. Best – keep watering regularly and do not break pattern; worst – never water.
4. Probably dry to wet, as plant may flourish.
5. Sudden change is usually worse because plants can adapt to slow change.
6. Put several plants in a greenhouse/laboratory and test their response(s); change watering, lighting, fertilizing cycles to test adaptation; some students may mention biotechnology.

Air Inventory (page 36)

1. Inside temperatures do not change much (depending on building's insulation); places near windows will change most.
2. Vent got colder/hotter to adjust (again, depending on insulation).
3. Yes, will have to keep changing; some day outside may be too hot/cold for system to handle properly.

Can We Control Climate? (page 38)

1. Air conditioned inside to hot outside.
2. Temperature of back of fridge/close to air conditioning unit (AC) – these machines make things cold but are really hot (themselves)!
3. AC is hotter – has to pull out hot air, so it gets hotter than surroundings.
4. AC takes away hot air and "dumps" it outside; heater adds hot air; insulation traps hot/cold air.
5. Turn it backwards; not built as heater, outside could freeze and break unit, will use more electricity than true heater
6. Refrigerator has pipes inside that pull hot air out from inside; pipes run to back and "dump" hot air to atmosphere; insulation in door and walls keep inside cool – class discussion.
7. NO!!!! For every amount of air to cool, refrigerator's back gets hot – hot air dumped back into room, plus heat from engine; will actually make room hotter.

How Does a Greenhouse Work? (page 40)

2. Probably open box – subject to most influence of surroundings.
3. Plastic covered one will get warmest because plastic is like greenhouse glass.

Clouds Over the Greenhouse (page 42)

2. Black; no, plants need sunlight to grow
3. Make up various greenhouses with these colors of glass; put plants inside and see which grow the best.
4. Less light gets in.
5. Night – no light.
6. Depending on measurements, perhaps a little cooler, but similar; total coverage will be most different; greenhouses still work when it is cloudy, just not as much.
7. If a lot of light is reflected out, greenhouse will not be as good; try with greenhouse model in a dusty room OR rig up a blower inside it and have dust blown around (2nd is better but more difficult); measure temperature over time.

Greenhouses are Traps (page 44)

2. Number of holes not as important as the fact that holes are present; more plastic will be warmer.
3. Box traps HEAT, air can move heat around; if greenhouse is hot enough and air circulation is gentle, unit will keep temperature, so yes both can be right.
4. Greenhouse effect under the glass, air becomes very hot and does not circulate – heat stroke.
5. City gets very hot, could dry out more or produce more clouds and become wetter.
6. Those with constant wind – coastal or mountainous; not in valley.

Humidity A (page 45)

1. Takes in heat: kettle takes in heat, water gets warmer (molecules move faster) and steam eventually forms.
2. Water takes in heat from hand, then evaporates and removes heat.
3. Water evaporates faster in dry environment (goes to where there is less of it) so the bowl in dry environment has less remaining water.
4. Body warmer than air (unless above 98°f/37°c) so water is heated by body and evaporates making you feel cold; less pronounced on humid days.
5. Too much water in air (humid), water on skin does not evaporate so no heat loss; may even be hard to towel dry if humid enough – feel warmer and maybe get light headed!
6. Hd/hw, hd/cw, hd/cd, hw/cw, hw/cd, cd/cw; hw/cd most extreme, hd/cd only temperature swing with no humidity effects.
7. Floods come with high humidity (rain); humidity came from somewhere, making that 'somewhere' dry; extreme weather evens out – Note some may remark that deserts can have flash floods – this is due to sudden rain on hard soil that does not drain.

Humidity B (page 48)

1. T will be same; w will be less in dry room.
2. No, "t" thermometer measures room temperature.
3. The larger the value of d, the drier; small d means it is humid.
4. It would not measure humidity.
5. Gets overall reading, not just in one place; average over all wind directions.
6. I) Put digital hygrometer and dry/wet bulb in same place; ii) measure across various humidities and write down value of d for % age with digital unit; iii) could see if trend graphs out (advanced answer).

Air in the Greenhouse (page 50)

2. c) Driest should be coldest; wettest should be hottest.
3. Makes it hotter; feels warmer; advanced answer – wet air holds more heat.
4. Plants; i) measure temperature in empty greenhouse over several days; ii) put in plants and measure temperature over several days; advanced method – how types of plants and/or number of plants affect readings.
5. Lots of plants, dense coverage; weather patterns that trap air; near large source of water (river, ocean); NO. The pacific northwest (i.e., Canada's Pacific Southwest) is a temperate rainforest – Note however, it is warmer than others at same latitude and rarely gets snow.

Carbon Dioxide and Greenhouses (page 53)

2. CO_2 will be warmer for some time period; may have up and down local change, but overall trend most important.
3. Vinegar and baking soda most CO_2, other set ups about the same CO_2; vinegar and baking soda most water vapor, vinegar median water vapor, no vinegar least water vapor; vinegar and baking soda warmest, vinegar median, no vinegar coolest.
4. CO_2 in atmosphere will increase temperature; advanced answer – CO_2 emission often comes with water vapor emission, which adds to warming.

A Natural Greenhouse (page 54)

1. Enclosed space, air, transparent roof, light source.
2. Humidity (water vapor), CO_2.
3. Oceans, plants source of water vapor; air, sky like a transparent "roof" that lets in sunlight and traps heat (atmosphere closes off Earth from space); CO_2 can add heat effect.
4. Drawing should label items in #3 – can be abstract.

The Color of Earth (page 55)

Colors on map: blue, green, brown, yellow, white . . .

2. White reflects sunlight best so you feel less hot.
3. Oceans are darker and so will get hotter; advanced students may remark that water reflects sunlight, but compare snowfield to water – former reflects in all directions, water only along one angle, so snow (Antarctica) is much more reflective than the oceans.
4. South America is darker due to the rainforests, so it traps more heat than a lighter colored desert as in North Africa; close to equator deserts are hot during the day because they receive a lot of sun and the *air* heats up. Class discussion - driest desert is in Antarctica (Vostok settlement).

Will the Earth Heat Evenly? (page 56)

1. Circle areas in the tropics and dark areas.
2. Probably got darker areas wrong – should mention darker things absorb more heat.
3. Forests are darker and trap more heat from sunlight. Greenland is white and reflects sunlight best, so it is colder.
4. Warm near the tropics and a few other areas (Gulf Stream) – again, oceans are dark so they absorb heat. Note they are not frozen on the coasts of Greenland, etc.
5. Africa for daytime temperature, but northern South America is closer to the equator!
6. Two regions about the same; northern Africa desert cools at night, South America rainforest traps heat.
7. Day – hot, lots of sun, reflects heat into air which gets very hot; night – all light has been reflected away, so gets very cold.
8. Darker areas, especially near the tropics; advanced students may note that warming will melt ice and snow, exposing more dark areas, so Greenland, etc. will get warmer.
9. Inside - make ground and buildings more reflective like deserts. Outside – everyone needs to help change lifestyle (lower co_2 emissions, etc.), Affected regions may be sources of food that get damaged by heating – people everywhere will have less to eat.

Water and Ice and Heat *(*page 59)

1 a) Open Ocean

b) Darkest, absorbs the most sunlight and therefore heats up.

2. (cold summer) (warm summer)

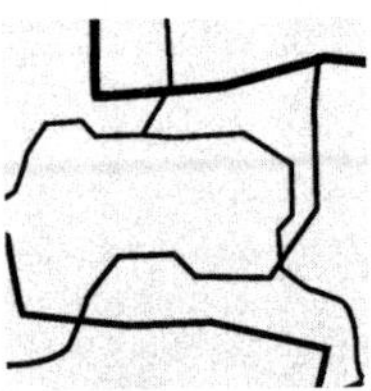 

3 a) (end of summer) (beginning of next summer)

b) (end of summer) (beginning of next summer)\

c) Usually ice refreezes in the dark winter, but if it stays warmer longer, there will not be enough time for it all to freeze over.

4. The Arctic will heat up because open ocean is dark and absorbs more heat from sunlight.
5. The change from total reflection to total absorption is very large ("dramatic change" in discussion); water now being heated instead of covered by ice will be sudden change to Arctic climate.

Feedback (page 60)

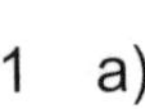

1 a) 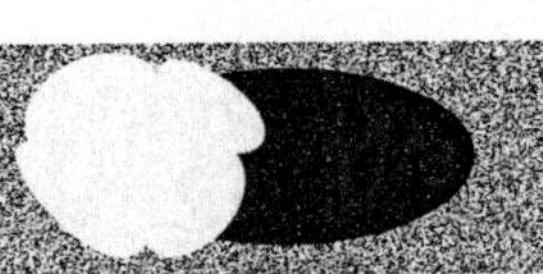 b) Picture A is warmer because it is overall darker.

2 a) 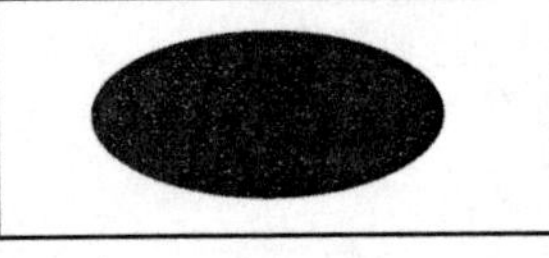 b) Picture C is colder because it has more white.

3. 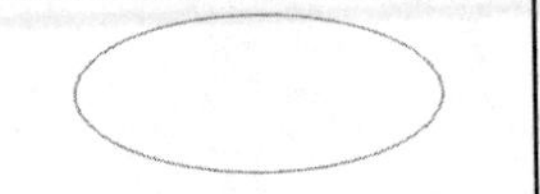

4 a) 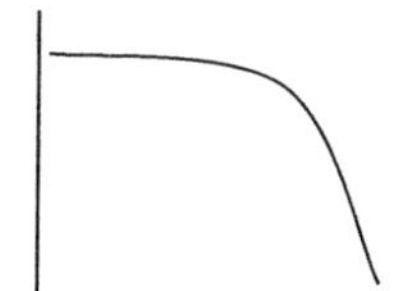

b) As the field becomes white it suddenly cools; key phrasing for feedback is "more and more." Acceptable if students draw straight line sloping down, but discuss why this curve is *more* correct.

5. When it gets cold, it snows. White snow reflects more sunlight and makes the scene even colder, so more snow falls. So it cools slowly then "more and more"/"faster and faster".

6. 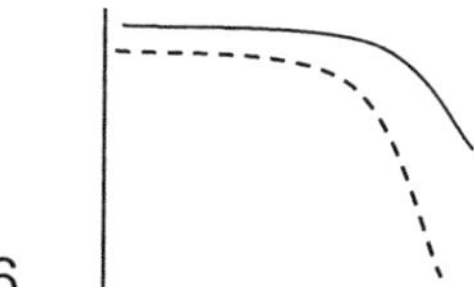

(Dashed line previous trend); it will take longer to get colder because the new start is just freezing)

7. 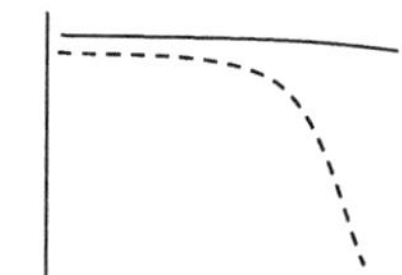

(Dashed line previous trend); if above freezing, no snow falls, and it will not get cold fast (possibly never stay below freezing) - this should warrant class discussion.

8. Dark ground with no snow exposed will absorb more heat, and gets darker as mud forms; no, if it thaws completely it cannot be called "permafrost" – class discussion.
9. Just a few degrees can be the difference between below freezing and above freezing; if winter stops being cold, plants will grow differently, animals will migrate differently, crops may grow differently; patterns will change and so will people's lives.

Moving Water in the Oceans (pages 64 - 65)

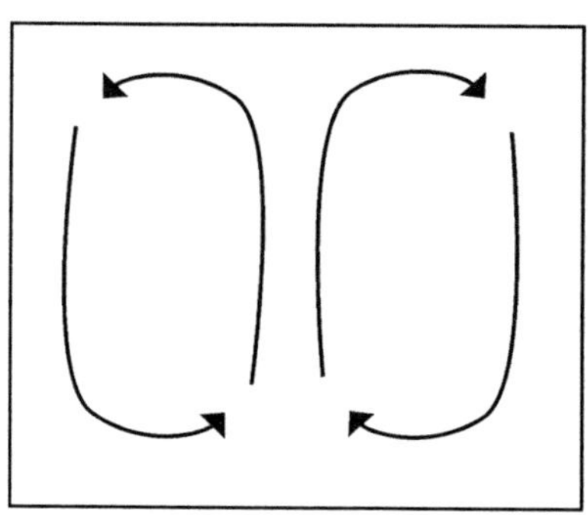

a) Water warmed at equator rises and goes northward; this cools and sinks to the ocean floor and travels back south where it warms again.

1. Paths are not straight because continents get in the way.
2. Water moving up or down, like in the cross-section of Atlantic
3. Cold water drops down deeply - it dives.
4. Follow the arrows.
5. Wow! That is so long! Earth is a big place and currents do not move so fast, so maybe it is not so surprising.
6. Conveyor moves trays/cars/etc. around – currents are like "belts" that move water around.

Changing the Current (page 67)

<u>Question in method:</u> Greenland does not get the red marbles, England gets from the south.

1. Glaciers/ice of Greenland.
2. Glaciers melting, releasing cold water into northern Atlantic; (global) warming can cause this.
3. Not as many red marbles make it to England – climate gets colder.
4. a) Maine will become warmer (red marbles collect perhaps).
   b) Spain will probably get hotter.
   c) Florida will probably stay the same.
5. Global warming can make some places hotter and other places colder, so everything changes.
6. Water, especially a whole ocean, does not cool that quickly; after a few seasons of colder temperatures, change "collects" and becomes sudden – advanced students mention feedback.

Rising Seas and Shores (page 69)

1. Small change in depth covers a large area (because the board is slanted).
2. Water surface is flat (still); at coast, ocean is level; so as water (ocean) gets deeper, the line of this level goes upward – "sea level" increases.
3. Answers will depend on students' angle of the board.
4. Streets will be underwater and foot of buildings – up to 2 stories (one story about 10 ft/3 m).
5. Places like southern Florida and the Netherlands will be completely underwater – lots of people there will have to move (tie in with *An Inconvenient Truth*).

Icebergs and Sea Level (page 70)

1. Glass 2 did not overflow.
2. The water overflows.
3. New icebergs – overflow the glass; icebergs already there are like glass 2 – the melt water fills the space taken up by the ice.

Glaciers and Sea Level (page 73)

1. The level stays about the same then suddenly gets deep fast.
2. When new ice cubes enter the water, the depth increases quickly because new ice cubes push water out of the way.
3. New ice cubes push the water out of the way, take up space so the depth/level increases; ice cubes already there melt and their water fills the space the ice took up so the level stays the same.
4. The left hand picture will have new ice enter the water and cause more increase in sea level.
5. Glaciers get lubricated ("oiled" or "made slippery") by melt water, slide easily into ocean; this is new ice so sea level could go up faster than scientists previously thought.

Relative Impact (page 75)

2. Largest five ice cubes in hot water in glass; smallest one ice cube in cold water in bucket; bucket has more water to cool, so it has least temperature change (alternatively, bucket contains more heat to melt ice).
3. Everything would heat up: most change in glass, least in bucket.
4. a) Large lakes can take more temperature change (like ice cube in bucket) so Boise stays warmer.
   b) Boise first; Milwaukee in long run because lake will slowly heat up and make climate warmer OR Boise becomes too hot (or cold) to live in.

Local Affects Global (page 77)

1. Different people will have slightly different times; Team C had longer to think about what to say and may have been fastest.
2. Answers will vary but probably the five second wait and spelling harder words; by slowing down one station, everybody gets backed up and the whole race takes longer (discussion to introduce concept of "bottleneck").
3. Local changes are like obstacles, so they can change the whole system; someone changing their local environment will change the global environment which can cause climate change; everyone is affected by climate change (including global warming).

Natural and Artificial (page 78)

In order of listing: N, A, N, A, A, N/A, N - steam in a bathroom forms because of natural processes - 'artificial' is in creating an environment that does not exist on its own naturally

1. Freezers are machines that make air cold. Snow from a freezer is artificial.
2. Water evaporates when it is warm. Clouds forming over warm water are natural.
3. Natural – the road is in a windy area. Artificial – the wind is caused by fast-moving cars.
4. CO_2 from factories/cars/buildings is artificial; volcanoes can emit CO_2 which is natural; feedback of snow can make it very cold and cause an Ice Age; a brighter sun can make it warm.

Sources and Sinks (page 80)

forest – sink, source if burned; ocean – sink; volcanoes – source; factories – source; cars – source; animals and people – source; limestone rocks – sink, source if dissolved or heated

1. Factories, volcanoes, forest fires can exhaust a lot of CO_2 quickly.
2. More volcanoes; the following forming and growing remove CO_2: plants, limestone, oceans.
3. Plant more trees, keep oceans healthy.
4. Invent material to remove CO_2, stop cars and factories from producing so much CO_2.
5. Faster – artificial; easier – probably natural; less expensive – probably natural; better – natural if done properly, but artificial could take less time.

Debating Pollution (page 81)

1. Pollution is a substance that is added to the environment in greater amounts than naturally there.
2. a) Bodies of water – no because clouds form from them naturally.
   b) Pools – yes because they are made by humans.
   c) Cars – yes because they are machines.
3. a) Volcanoes – no because they erupt and smoke naturally.
   b) Factories – yes because they are built and used by humans.
   c) Forest fires – yes if human started, no if lightning/volcano.

4 a) Forests absorb sunlight to heat up; release CO_2 in fires; release water vapor.
   b) Clouds form from released water vapor; plants pull in CO_2 from atmosphere.

5. Because of human activity like starting forest fires, it is possible for a natural thing to become a source of pollution ; a sudden volcanic eruption could be considered pollution - it is abnormal.
9. Yes! Debates get people thinking and produce ideas to help solve problems.

An Inconvenient Truth Graphing (page 83)

1. Forests in northern hemisphere taking in CO_2 then releasing it in the autumn ("breathing").
2. Temperature increased with CO_2 increase; temperature decreased with CO_2 decrease.
3. Graphs match up exactly – evidence is strong.
4. Temperature will go up because CO_2 has gone up.
5. Show that when CO_2 increases the temperature increases; compare measurements several years ago to now; yes, that evidence exists. (weather balloon measurements)

Are Clouds Good or Bad? (page 84)

1. Colder, sun not shining through.
2. Clouds will increase in number because there will be more warm water.
3. Land will get cooler; oceans will get cooler – so it may stop making clouds (start another Feedback discussion).
4. Moist land becomes dry – drought; clouds that form make rain elsewhere and could cause flooding; advanced students may note that dry land, if rained on, will flood (desert rains in Arizona).
5. Clouds themselves are not good or bad; changing how many form and where they may go because of climate change can be good or bad for people.

Cities and Climate (page 85)

1. Cars, factories, animals, people, buildings
2. Water ways, swimming pools, cars, factories, animals, people, plants, buildings
3. Plants, water
4. Ground, plants, animals, people, factories, buildings
5. Cities get a lot of blame because of factories, cars, buildings, and people.
6. Limit factories and cars; plant more trees; build artificial lakes; invent CO_2 removal machines.
7. Only indoor swimming pools (or cover in day); limit factories and cars; recycle water from air.
8. Build levees/dikes; build away from shore; put buildings on stilts; yes, good idea because it is always better to be prepared than to wait for emergency.
9. Closed – reflects sunlight and cools; open – light comes in and heats rooms; with good insulation and air circulation can keep warm like with blankets and cool like loose clothing.
10. Cost saved in heating/cooling bills in long run; first efforts always more expensive – building more becomes less expensive because designs are no longer "special" (good class discussion).